The Madame MacAdam Travelling Theatre

This is a hugely entertaining, funny play about an English theatre company which gets stuck without petrol in a small southern Irish town in the middle of the Second World War. The play tells several stories, of young love, of the painting of a greyhound to win a race, of a young child lost and found. But most of all it tells of the wonderful Madame MacAdam and her troupe and of the comic and tragic effects that they have upon an isolated community.

The Madame MacAdam Travelling Theatre was first performed by Field Day Theatre Company in a ten week production touring Ireland, beginning in Derry on 9th September 1991. It was presented at the Dublin Theatre Festival in October.

Thomas Kilroy's plays include **The Death and Resurrection of Mr Roche** (Dublin Theatre Festival, 1968, transferred to Hampstead Theatre, London); **The O'Neill** (Peacock Theatre, Dublin, 1969); **Tea and Sex and Shakespeare** (Abbey Theatre, Dublin, 1976); **Talbot's Box** (Dublin Theatre Festival, 1977, transferred to Royal Court Theatre, London); **Double Cross** (Field Day Theatre Company touring production, 1986, transferred to Royal Court Theatre, London) and **The Madame MacAdam Travelling Theatre** (Field Day Theatre Company touring production, 1991). He has translated Chekhov's **The Seagull** (Royal Court Theatre, London, 1981) and Ibsen's **Ghosts** (Dublin Theatre Festival, 1989) and in 1971 he published a novel, **The Big Chapel**, which was awarded the Guardian Fiction Prize and the Heinemann Award for Literature and was shortlisted for the Booker Prize. He lives in Co Mayo in the West of Ireland and is a director of the Field Day Theatre Company.

Methuen New Theatrescripts series offers frontline intelligence of the most original and exciting work from the fringe:

The Madame MacAdam Travelling Theatre

A play by
Thomas Kilroy

Methuen Drama

A Methuen New Theatrescript

First published in Great Britain in 1991 by Methuen Drama,
Michelin House, 81 Fulham Road, London SW3 6RB and
distributed in the United States of America by HEB Inc.,
361 Hanover Street, Portsmouth, New Hampshire
NH 03801 3959.

Copyright © 1991 Thomas Kilroy

The author has asserted his moral rights

ISBN 0-413-66310-8

A CIP catalogue record for this book is available from the
British Library.

The illustration on the front cover is 'A Bene-fit', published by
Thomas McLean in 1826, and is reproduced by courtesy of the Board
of Trustees of the Victoria & Albert Museum.

Typeset in 10 on 11pt Linotron Baskerville
by Hewer Text Composition Services, Edinburgh
Printed and bound in Great Britain
by Cox & Wyman Ltd, Cardiff Road, Reading

For Julie

Characters

Members of the MacAdam Company:

Madame MacAdam
Lyle Jones, *a principal actor*
Sally, *an actress*
Rabe, *an actor*
Simon, *driver, general factotum*

Townspeople:

The Sergeant of the Gardaí (*Police*)
Marie Therese, *his daughter*
Jo, *her pal*
Bun Bourke, *town baker and Squad Leader of LDF (Home Guard)*

Other townspeople:

Chamberlain, *a black marketeer and dog-trainer*
Young Maher, *a townsman*
Slipper, *a dog handler*
LDF Men

The character of **Chamberlain** can be doubled with **Lyle Jones** or **Bun Bourke**.

The actor playing **Young Maher** also plays **Simon** and **Slipper**.

The Madame MacAdam Travelling Theatre is a small English touring company of players. It arrives in a provincial Irish town, sometime in the early 1940s.

The Madame MacAdam Travelling Theatre was first performed by Field Day Theatre Company in a ten week production touring Ireland, beginning in Derry on 9th September 1991, and presented at the Dublin Theatre Festival on 15th October, with the following cast:

Madame MacAdam	Helen Ryan
Lyle Jones	Julian Curry
Sally	Amanda Hurwitz
Rabe	Tom Radcliffe
Simon	Donagh Deeney
The Sergeant	Kevin Flood
Marie Therese	Tina Kelleher
Jo	Fionnuala Murphy
Bun Bourke	Conor McDermottroe
Chamberlain	Conor McDermottroe
Young Maher	Donagh Deeney
Slipper	Donagh Deeney

Directed by Jim Nolan
Designed by Monica Frawley
Lighting by Conleth White

Note

The text of the play as printed may differ from that of
performance.

Part One

Scene One

Music. Projection: **The World at War! Enter Madame MacAdam. The lost child. And the doctoring of a dog.**

A dark stage. Distant sound of a bomber approaching, passing overhead, passing away. Lights of a chugging vehicle across, back. It approaches audience, headlights swinging through the auditorium. Engine dies. Headlights off. The side of a van now towards the audience. Momentary pause. Rising light. The side of the van is brightly painted with the company name emblazoned on it: **The Madame MacAdam Travelling Theatre.**

Momentary pause. The side of the van facing audience swings open. **Madame MacAdam** *in flowered kimono-style gown is on stage, before the footlights.*

Madame MacAdam (*to audience*) Ladies and Gentlemen! Tonight we will offer the usual fare. A love story. A lost child. Villainy at large. While in the background the drums of war. And at the end, that frail salvation of the final curtain. What else is there?

My troup is decimated. We have lost our indifferent Claudius and obese Gertrude together with a fifth-rate Horatio in a town called, I believe, Mullingar. Together, I may add, with most of our petrol. Dreadful place, really, Mullingar. Positively decorated with cow-dung. You may well ask how I, Madame MacAdam, am so reduced? To tell you the truth, m'dears, from the moment we set out on this dreadful tour we have been beset by the malignant deities. I exaggerate. One needs to exaggerate to keep banality at bay. Tickets half a crown, one and sixpence in the back rows. The question is: What frenzy, what compulsion is this? To display ourselves nightly as others before others? To costume ourselves? Is it simply exhibitionism? The other question, of course is this: What on earth are we doing here? Do you know, I believe we simply reached a crossroads somewhere in Ulster. Someone mentioned the Free State. The name beckoned. So here we are! And yet, yet again I feel the suffusion in my veins, the quickening of the powers. Can it be that in this remote, indeed barbaric corner of Eirer I am about to reach towards the flaming tablets once more? Who knows? Time alone will tell.

Van side swings shut on **Madame MacAdam**.

Lights down. Lights up: night.

Enter a line of Local Defence Force (LDF: Home Guard) led by **Squadron Leader Bourke**, *otherwise the town baker, a fat man with an agitated moustache.*

Bourke Company! Halt! Prepare to examine ve-hic-al. On guard, men. Take no chances. Remember there's a war on now. This could be it, lads. The start of the invasion.

1st LDF Man Sure it's only the travelling amusements, Bun. They arrived a couple of nights ago.

2nd LDF Man That's right, Bun.

3rd LDF Man We can go home, so.

Bourke (*extreme patience*) Corporal Foley! Attention! Two steps forward. At the double. Halt! (*Explosion.*) Listen, you fuckin' eedjit. Don't call me Bun. D'ya hear! In this uniform I'm not Bun Bourke. I'm Squad Leader Bourke. Be day I may be a baker but be night I'm officer in charge of this Squad.

1st LDF Man Sure I was only saying what we all know.

Bourke Listen, Foley, I don't give a tuppenny shit what you're saying. We all know nothing – nothing. Is that understood?

1st LDF Man But the name is on the side of the lorry there! Look it!

Bourke That remains to be seen. Where's that child that's missing, hah?

1st LDF Man She'll turn up.

2nd LDF Man Sure the guards is out looking for her.

Bourke Everyone in the town should be out searching for her. Where is she, hah? Hour of night. Day after day. What does it mean? That's what I want to know. Hah? Anyways. Right now, boy, we're in uniform, do yis know what it is to be in uniform, boy? Members of the Local Defence Force engaged in manoeuvres with the whole fuckin' country under possible attack. (*Heavy irony.*) I'm only saying what we all know. Jasus. Boy, you're going to be the right fuckin' eedjit when the Jerries arrive. And the Tommies arrive. And the Yanks arrive. Never mind the fuckin' Japs. Oh, I'm only saying what we all know! Get back to your place. No! Stop! Corporal Foley. Present arms. One, two, three. About-turn, forward march. Left-right, left-right, left-right. Halt! Right, lads, now. At the double. Surround the ve-hic-al, arms at the ready. Prepare to take prisoners if necessary. Note down all marks of identification and we'll report back to the guards' barracks.

Bourke, *crouching run, leads some of the others off, around the back of the van.*

3rd LDF Man God Almighty. What time is it?

4th LDF Man It's gone ten o'clock.

3rd LDF Man I'm perished. I'm going home to hell out of this.

4th LDF Man Sure you can't do that. You'll be courtmartialled, so you will.

3rd LDF Man Courtmartialled me arse. We're out with that lunatic five nights a week and at all hours looking for Germans in henhouses. It's beyond in the Dardonellies he ought to be. Are ya coming or going?

4th LDF Man I'm staying. Amn't I on duty.

3rd LDF Man Duty away with you till the cows come home. I'm off. (*Exits.*)

4th LDF Man Oh, Lord! We're a man short now if 'tis the invasion.

He follows the others behind the van: empty stage. **Marie Therese**, *very pretty, and* **Jo**, *very plain with heavy spectacles, both about sixteen or seventeen, come on with their bicycles.* **Jo** *is carrying a shopping bag. The sound of the plane returns, passing overhead, engine spluttering. The two girls drop the bicycles and look up: night light.*

Marie Therese (*jumping up and down*) It's Jerry all right. I know it! I just know it!

Jo 'Tis like he's lost.

Marie Therese Oh, God, Jo, I wish I was above with your man in that aireyplane!

Jo It's monstrous, that's what it is. Killing people.

Marie Therese I'd go with him to the ends of the earth so I would.

Jo Marie Therese, there's limits, alas. The average range of a twin-engined bomber, I do believe, is twelve hundred miles, give or take. Besides. You haven't a word of German so you haven't.

Marie Therese How do you know who he is up there? Snotty! Anyways. At times there's no need, y'know, to say a word. Just looks is enough. Glances. Course you wouldn't know about such things, Jo – (*No answer.*) God there are times when I could kill ya! Yor just an auld stick, so y'are.

The plane has gone off.

Jo I'd like to have a baby.

Marie Therese God Almighty! Such a thing to say! It's no wonder y'are the way y'are.

Jo (*tight control*) I don't wish to discuss the matter any further, thank you very much.

Marie Therese (*quick shift*) Promise not to tell, Jo! Cross your heart! I'm going to go off with that stage crowd beyond when they leave. Run away. I'll be able to dress up! D'ya think I should pluck me eyebrows?

Jo If you pluck them any more you'll be down to the subsoil. Besides. You said the very same thing last year when that crowd was here, the Daniels Variety Show. 'Member?

Marie Therese God, do you think there might be a fella in the show like that fella last year? Wasn't he only gorgeous?

Jo *bursts into tears.*

Marie Therese Ah, Jo!

Jo (*tears*) 'Tisn't that. It's only. I was thinking. I was only thinking of me mother and father beyond in England in that factory with all them bombs dropping.

Marie Therese But, sure, they'll be all right.

Jo (*tears*) Who says?

Marie Therese Daddy says –

Jo (*tears. Dismissive*) Daddy says –

Marie Therese Daddy says they have bomb shelters in England under all the streets and that everyone fits into them. (*Grabbing* **Jo**'s *shopping bag*.) What have you got in that ould bag anyways?

Jo (*panic*) No, don't touch that! Give it to me.

Marie Therese (*rifling*) What're you hiding? Bits of bread. And a bottle of milk. Who for? Are ya going on a picnic or wha'?

Jo Give it to me!

Marie Therese What for?

Jo It's – supplies.

Marie Therese And an auld towel. (*Teacher's voice.*) What's the meaning of this, miss?

Jo Mind your own business.

Jo *grabs her bag of belongings.*

Marie Therese They're going to take you into the asylum one of these days.

Jo Leave me alone!

Marie Therese Stay there then. Pimply face!

Marie Therese *exits with her bicycle.* **Jo** *hugs her bag to herself.*

Jo (*eyes closed, rocking on her heels*) Turn out the light. No-one see. Mammy take care of baby in the dark. Always there. I did it, don't care. I did it, Sergeant. I don't care, don't care. I stole her. Stole the child. Little Nellie Lannigan.

Blackout.

Lights up. Table and chairs, mantelpiece and wireless: the kitchen of the **Sergeant**'s *house. The* **Sergeant** *is unbuttoning his tunic, removing his cap.* **Chamberlain** *and* **Slipper** *stand in front of him,* **Slipper** *holding a muzzled greyhound.* **Chamberlain** *has a tic of constantly looking over his shoulder.* **Slipper** *is moronic, wears wellingtons with the tops rolled down and is an expert dog-handler.*

Chamberlain Parade the bitch, Slipper, in front of the Sergeant.

Slipper *and dog parade.*

Sergeant (*looking closely*) It's miraculous no other word for it, Chamberlain.

Chamberlain (*producing dog-card*) There we are. Dixie's Wonder by Wonder Boy out of Rose Marie. Certified.

Sergeant Poor Dixie. That poor hoor Dixie.

Chamberlain She's dead and buried, Sergeant.

Sergeant I'll miss that bitch, Chamberlain. She's lying out there in the back yard, God rest her.

Chamberlain (*quick glance over shoulder*) That one's gone, this one's here. Dixie resurrected, brought back to life by human handiwork and the fortunate discovery of a near lookalike below in me own litter. Am I right or am I wrong, Dr Watson?

Sergeant (*bending to look*) Matched to a T. Tell us, Chamberlain, how did you get the colours right?

Chamberlain (*glance over shoulder*) Now-now, Sergeant! You're the law round here and I'm the criminal. It'd be better for you and it'd be better for me and it'd be better for that poor gaum Slipper there if I said no more. But I'll say this – the basic ingredients is axle-grace and black-lead.

Sergeant Lord save us and will it ever come off again?

Chamberlain I can tell you it won't come off while she's doing thirty twenty-five round Clonmel track. Provided. Provided she breaks well. If she breaks bad we're all down in the poorhouse in Thomastown. Am I right, Tonto? Now here's the gist of it. Once she's first past the post every bookie in Clonmel will go loco. Where's the bitch? Sure everyone knows Dixie couldn't race from one side of the road to the other if she were fed a deliberate diet of blancmange and rump steak. But where's this bitch? Give us a look at her! She's gone!

Sergeant Gone?

Chamberlain Vamoose.

Sergeant But where?

Chamberlain The man asks me where! The man wants to know! She came in off the track. Right there, Slipper? But she never made it to the killings. No bitch. No law. Am I right, Inspector?

Sergeant But where is she?

Chamberlain England.

Sergeant England!

Chamberlain Well she is and she isn't.

Sergeant How so?

Chamberlain (*quick glance over shoulder*) Here's how, Officer. All we've got to do is get one of these actor fellas here to come to the track with us. Pretending to be an English buyer, y'see, over from Wembley. She wins, he buys. Once the race is over he goes back to his acting with the disguise removed. The bitch goes back to me own yard, with the colour gone as an unreg-istered sapling that never went round a track in all her born days, her innocent little pawsie-pawsies shining white for inspection by all and sundry. And Dixie? Everyone will think Dixie's gone over the water like many a one before her, God save us all –

Sergeant (*dismissively*) Not at all –

Chamberlain Oh yes at all. Amn't I right, General Custer?

Sergeant And how in the name of God would one of the actors do such a thing?

Chamberlain Sure all he has to do is put on a crombie and one of them posh accents.

Sergeant But *why* would he do it?

Chamberlain Petrol.

Sergeant Petrol?

Chamberlain Ay, petrol. They've been scouring the country-side for petrol, the actors. And Yours Truly will provide.

Sergeant You mean the black market, Chamberlain?

Chamberlain You said it, Sergeant. They're your words, not mine.

Sergeant Petrol! (*Pause.*) We're finished if we're caught.

Chamberlain Caught! Sure you know yourself, Sergeant that no-one ever gets caught in this country.

Sergeant (*hurt*) Ah now that's not true, Chamberlain. Didn't I lock up many a man in my time?

Enter **Marie Therese**.

Sergeant And where have you been, miss, until this hour of the night? Were you near that theatre crowd beyond?

Marie Therese No I wasn't. I was out on the bike with Jo.

Sergeant Look at the time it is there on the clock.

Marie Therese I know the time it is, Daddy, there on the clock.

Sergeant Riding a bike around in the dark! And don't be giving back-answers either, miss.

Marie Therese Ah, Daddy! I'm not an infant, y'know.

Sergeant Have you done your exercises for school in the morning?

Marie Therese I did me exercises ages ago. (*Tears.*) Why don't you treat me right when others are listening? Like a grown-up person? I'm not a child any more, y'know!

A banging overhead. All look up.

Sergeant God Almighty, that's your mother off again! Will you go up to her, Marie Therese, there's a good girl and see what's up with her?

Marie Therese I'm going to me own room, so I am. 'Tis the only place in this house I can have peace and quiet. (*Sob.*) There's plenty of opportunities for a girl like me in San Francisco, so there is! (*She exits.*)

Sergeant It's only me nerves, Chamberlain.

Chamberlain Don't I know it, Sergeant.

Sergeant I wouldn't harm a hair on her head.

Chamberlain Look who's talkin'! Saint Anthony isn't in it.

Sergeant There's times I feel this uniform melting into me skin. I was never cut out for this job, Chamberlain.

Chamberlain God Almighty, don't talk of resigning, Sergeant. Do you want us all in Mountjoy Jail?

Sergeant And now this little child missing in the town. Little Nellie Lannigan. Only five years of age. Now who'd want to steal away a little child, I wonder? Them actor people? Not at all! Though I grant you some of them may be a bit, y'know, mixum-gatherum.

Chamberlain Tell us, Sergeant, did you ever see a travelling show be the name of Bam-bam-boozulum? Miss Henrietta

Morgan, the Australian Personality Girl? Angus McCraig
and his Twelve Accordians each one a different size to the
next one down to the size of a matchbox? Oh the melodies of
that Scotchman!

Sergeant It's a mystery to me, the same theatricals. The
worst yokoboko of all is the lad that invites you up on the
stage beside him.

Chamberlain Is it the magician, Sergeant?

Sergeant Or it could be just to answer questions like when
you're in a sorta trance. Mesmer. He's the real dangerman.
I'll tell you one thing and it's no lie, Chamberlain. What goes
on up on that stage and what goes on down here is different
things entirely.

They meditate upon this.

Lights down.

Scene Two

Music. Projection: **Curtain-up! An Investigation Begins. And
the Art of Acting is Explained.**

Lights up.

Backstage: dressing-table, large mirror. **Madame MacAdam** *and*
Lyle Jones *finishing make-up and costuming for the play that is to
follow.* **Madame** *is in eighteenth century servant costume and* **Lyle**,
*sixtyish, is made-up as the young Robert Emmet, the eighteenth century
Irish patriot.*

Lyle Jones Do we have a good house? Are we packing them
in? Do you know, I believe these people adore the theatre.
Have never played before such splendid audiences in me life.
Never. Promise.

Madame MacAdam You are quite, quite remarkable.

Lyle Jones Thank you.

Madame MacAdam You know perfectly well that I do not intend that as a compliment.

Lyle Jones Mumsie! Please! Don't be cross with me. Not now. Not before curtain. Shan't be able to get me lines –

Madame MacAdam You've been saying the same thing nightly for twenty-five years. Splendid audiences, indeed!

Lyle Jones One must say the same thing nightly. Otherwise one is unable to go on.

Madame MacAdam I blame myself. I have simply lost control over everything.

Lyle Jones Nonsense, darling. Things have been infinitely worse in days gone by. My God, we've been through every conceivable mishap you and I! What more can happen to us?

Madame MacAdam You actually believe that, don't you? That things get better.

Lyle Jones But, of course –

Madame MacAdam Whereas the truth is that something quite dreadful has been wearing us down for years now. We seem to be dwindling. It's rather like a wasting sickness. Soon there will be nothing left of us.

Lyle Jones (*outburst*) I simply will not allow you to speak like that! Won't! Won't! Won't!

Madame MacAdam I have this sense of imminent collapse while at the same time the prospect of great illumination. Very odd.

Lyle Jones (*seizing it*) Illumination! Absolutely! (*Drawing himself up.*) Whatever it is, let us rise to the challenge. Oh, for heaven's sake, we still perform, don't we? People still come to see us. Why worry about anything else? We do not starve. Though, mind you, we'd better find some petrol jolly soon. I will make enquiries among the natives.

Madame MacAdam You will do no such thing!

Lyle Jones Sorreee! Won't be a naughty boy. Promise!

Madame MacAdam We have lost half the company. We are reduced to five counting Simon who is incapable of speech.

Lyle Jones But the boy Rabe and the girl Sally are terribly good, terribly good. Though she will insist upon standing in front of me when I'm in full flight. Must speak to her, dear. Question of status. Boy Rabe is good. Trifle unsteady, perhaps. But goodish, goodish.

Madame MacAdam Rabe is *superb*! Even in our most ludicrous moments he is electrifying upon the stage.

Lyle Jones I shouldn't exaggerate, dear. Good potential, yes. Needs coaching. Bad posture.

Madame MacAdam Rubbish. His kind do not require posture. Electrifying!

Lyle Jones Promising, yes.

Madame MacAdam Electrifying!

Lyle Jones I wish you wouldn't repeat yourself, dear. Gives me the willies.

Madame MacAdam Lyle Jones! Where are our dreams? The heights that we once aspired to? Have we allowed the nightly grind to wear us down? Have we surrendered to mediocre repetition?

Lyle Jones But, my dear, you have always said that we must trust in what we have, what we are, that there is nothing else. You are the one who speaks of accepting our talent, whatever it is – great or small –

Madame MacAdam Yes, I do believe that –

Lyle Jones I have devoted my life to that principle. Everything that I have I have given to you.

Madame MacAdam Yes, I know. Perhaps I am simply tired.

Lyle Jones But, of course. (*Puts his arm about her shoulders.*) You simply take on too much, you know. I have been frightfully concerned for you.

Madame MacAdam Oh, Lyle Jones, stop it at once! When this abominable tour has ended I shall devote my life to the development of the inner consciousness.

Lyle Jones (*real distress*) My God, you can't mean that! What shall become of me? I am utterly helpless without you, you know that. I should cease to function if you were not about.

There is a burst of wild applause off.

Madame MacAdam That is our cue. Time to join the others. Come along.

Lyle Jones Mumsie, I am so very frightened. Look at my hands how they shake!

Madame MacAdam Place your hand upon my arm and it will not shake.

He does so and they make a dignified exit together into the applause which then dies down.

Piano music: **Madame MacAdam** *in full voice, the Thomas Moore melody 'Silent O Moyle'.*

Lights up. The sides of the van have been opened up to reveal a stage and proscenium, footlights. We are backstage. One or two pieces of stage shrubbery. **Sally**, *attractive but hard, in her late twenties, is playing* *the part of Sarah Curran, the eighteenth century Irish heroine. Sarah is in her garden in the moonlight dreaming of her lover, the young, eighteenth century Irish revolutionary Robert Emmet. Setting 1805. The company is performing the playlet to the townspeople. Offstage,* **Madame MacAdam** *finishes her song at the piano, over Sarah Curran's first speech. Then she enters as Annie Devlin, Sarah Curran's Irish maid.*

Rabe *and* **Simon**, *in red-coat military costume and bored, are smoking cigarettes to one side, backstage.*

Out, beyond, is an unseen but boisterous audience of townspeople in the darkness. Catcalls and cries of 'shush' punctuate the performances.

Sally (*as Sarah Curran*) Oh, Robert! This night shall see thy fate unfold. And mine, too, alas. I know thy dream, to free Ireland from the Saxon yoke. (*Applause from audience.*) But what of thy dear Sarah? Oh, Providence, guide me this night. Hark! Who's there? Annie! I thought it might be – He!

Madame MacAdam (*as Annie Devlin*) Sure I know who it is you thought it might be. Is it Mr Robert Emmet? (*Cheers.*)

Sally Hush! Do not speak his name. The Castle spies are everywhere.

Madame MacAdam But he's waiting below.

Sally Who? He?

Madame MacAdam The man himself.

Sally Show him up! Quickly! Quickly! (**Madame MacAdam** *off.*) Now be brave, Sarah Curran, be brave!

Cries from 'audience': 'Good girl yourself, Sarah Curran.' 'Shut up out of that, with you!'

Enter **Lyle Jones**, *principal actor, as Robert Emmet with* **Madame** *as Annie in attendance.*

Lyle Jones (*as Robert Emmet*) Sarah!

Sally Robert! (*Tears.*)

Madame MacAdam (*aside to 'audience'*) I think 'tis time for me to be off out of here. (*Exits to one or two yells.*)

Lyle Jones What? Am I to give thee courage? Come, now!

Sally Oh, Robert, I feel thou hast some deadly message for me –

Lyle Jones (*low, intense*) Yes. Yes. Tomorrow, tomorrow –

Sally Tomorrow? So soon? Oh, Robert, what can you do with a handful of men?

Lyle Jones (*out*) With a handful of men Napoleon freed France. With a handful of men Cortez conquered Mexico. With a handful of men Cromwell seized the House of Commons. With a handful of men I shall free Ireland from England! (*'Audience' uproar, shouts, hand-clapping, pounding of heels on the floor.*)

Madame MacAdam (*off*) Help! Fly away, Mr Emmet. The soldiers are coming.

Madame MacAdam *on, in the grip of the two redcoats played by* **Rabe** *and* **Simon**.

Madame MacAdam The house is surrounded, Miss Sarah.

Lyle Jones (*aside*) My fears are realized.

Madame MacAdam Take your dirty hands off me or I'll knock your block off.

She is released and exits to cheers and laughs from the 'audience'. When off, she discards her cloak. She is now wearing a shining green costume. She puts on a tiara and seats herself at the piano.

Sally Stay, good officer. There is some mistake.

Lyle Jones No, there is no mistake. I have been betrayed by those nearest to me. Is it not ever the story of Irish patriots? Well, Major Sirr, we meet at last –

Rabe (*as Major Sirr*) Robert Emmet, I arrest you in the name of His Majesty, on the charge of High Treason. Take him! (*Boos from 'audience'.*)

Sally (*around* **Lyle Jones**'s *knees*) No, Robert!

Lyle Jones My dear – it is a far, far better thing that I do, than I have ever done; it is a far, far better rest that I go – (*Wrong play: quick change.*) No! Think only of this when I am gone. When my country takes its place among the nations of the earth – then and not till then shall my epitaph be written –

As he is led off, **Madame MacAdam** *strikes up and sings 'She is far from the land where her young hero sleeps'.* **Sally** *swoons on the stage.* **Simon** *pushes the piano, together with* **Madame**, *on stage, to applause. The van closes up.* **Lyle Jones** *and* **Rabe** *emerge around the side. They are now 'backstage'.*

Lyle Jones But, my dear boy, we actors are the creation of our audiences. They create us nightly. We exist only in their imaginations. When they walk out of the theatre we cease to exist. We become nonentities once more. Just like everyone else. (*Pause.*) Besides. You were, as always, quite splendid on stage.

Rabe (*gritted*) Do not patronize me. I will not be patronized.

Lyle Jones Rabe – Please. Why cannot we speak to one another with some degree of decency?

Rabe You don't even see it. How extraordinary! He doesn't even see the rubbish he's in.

Lyle Jones Rubbish? But the Irish simply adore these Hibernian melodramas.

Rabe The sheer vulgarity of it!

Lyle Jones Vulgarity fiddlesticks. I am as perfect in this as I am in *Hamlet*.

Rabe We're bitched. Why not admit to it? Eh? I simply cannot stand it when people will not face up to the truth.

Lyle Jones You are tired, darling. Overwrought.

Rabe Look. I can't abide half-measures. Always settling for compromise. Not for me, thank you. Either you go for the whole kit and caboodle or it's not worth it.

Lyle Jones Later in the week we shall do my Othello. You'll be Iago. Promise.

Rabe With what? A cast of five? What a laugh. My head is splitting. I keep having these most dreadful headaches. And I have this absolute certainty that if we hang about here much longer we're going to – (*Stop*.) Forgot! We have no more bloody petrol!

Lyle Jones Rabe. You know how we care for you –

Rabe I took this tour for Madame in there. I'd never heard anyone talk about theatre the way she does.

Lyle Jones But we're both thrilled to have you in the company, dear. Thrilled.

Rabe I know you took me in. I know the state I was in. I know all that. I know I should be grateful.

Lyle Jones Please. Not a word! Grateful? Nonsense.

Rabe It was the way she talked. She made it sound as if theatre could heal everything, make it whole again. Well, where is it, then? This great fucking theatre of transformation? It's ghastly, that's what it is. We're reduced to tat. We've lost half the company. And all our petrol.

Lyle Jones Not to worry. Everything will be hunky-dory. Just you wait and see.

Rabe How?

Lyle Jones I am putting my mind to it.

Rabe Christ! The Irish are going to screw us. You do know that, don't you?

Lyle Jones What matters is that we perform. Nothing else matters, really. If we continue to do that everything will come right in the end. Always has for me. Do you know, there were moments out there, even tonight, when I felt the frisson, downtrodden people under the yoke, rising to throw off the oppressor –

Rabe It's just shit, mate. Absolute shit.

Lyle Jones Temper.

Rabe (*he regrets it as he says it but cannot help himself*) You're just second-rate. That's all. (*Pause. Violently.*) Go on! Say it. Say that I'm treacherous.

Lyle Jones I wouldn't dream of such a thing.

Rabe What's the matter with me? I don't know what's the matter with me. I'm just full of shit. Please pay no attention to me.

Lyle Jones Well. Well, I must say. Well, since we're on the subject of shit –

Rabe Look, I am sorry –

Lyle Jones No! May I say that your conduct is quite appalling. The way you tart about the place. Dropping your trousers before every whore along the way, every little bitch in heat you have to have it. Positively disgusting so it is the way you go on. Revolting, filthy little pig you are –

Rabe and **Lyle Jones** *confront one another, briefly. Then* **Rabe** *promptly disappears around the side of the van.*

Lyle Jones Rabe – please! I am sorry. Oh God. I always do it, always the bloody mess. Stupid, stupid old fool what have you done?

Head in hands. Head up, erect he follows **Rabe** *off.*

Marie Therese *and* **Jo**, *with their bicycles, emerge out of the darkness on their way home from the show.*

Marie Therese God, did you see your man? All the time he was up on that stage his eyes were boring into me. I could have died.

Jo It's an optical illusion.

Marie Therese A wha'?

Jo I'm only being – punctilious. Besides. Young Maher is still following us.

Marie Therese Where?

Young Maher *slides into view, aged thirty-something, evasive, sly, dirty-minded, hands in his pockets.*

Young Maher Hey! Will you take down your knickers for me, young one? Down in the bushes?

Marie Therese Jesus, Mary and Joseph, did you hear that? (*To* **Young Maher**.) I'm going to tell me father on you. He'll lock you up in the barracks, boy.

Young Maher Your father'll be arrested himself one of these days. Isn't he always losing money on them greyhounds?

Marie Therese (*tears*) That's not true. Oh, Mammy.

Jo Help! Help! We're being assaulted by young Maher. Help!

Marie Therese (*dry-eyed*) Shut up, Jo, or someone'll hear you, so they will.

Enter **Rabe** *at a trot still in his stage costume.*

Rabe Yes? Yes? What is it?

Marie Therese Oh, it's him! I'm going weak at the knees!

Jo (*pointing*) It's that fellow. He's at us.

Marie Therese (*gush*) Oh don't take any notice of him. Really. I have to put up with it all the time. I saw you in the play, you were great, I suppose I shouldn't say that now so I shouldn't, are you staying long? Don't mind that corner boy there. He's always following me. I'm going every night to the plays with me father. Me father is Sergeant of the guards. This is my best friend Jo. I'm Marie Therese.

Jo Us. He's always following us.

Rabe All right. That's it, then. On your way, mate.

Jo Go home, young Maher, when that man tells you to.

Marie Therese (*adult*) Jo. Leave it to between the men.

Young Maher Dirty fuckin' foreigners! Bun Bourke knows all about you, boy. Bun Bourke'll take care of yous. (*He exits.*)

Rabe (*agitated*) What? What is this? What is he saying? What does he mean? It's the first warning. I knew it. We must leave here.

Marie Therese Oh this town'll be the death of me yet, such carry-on and in front of the visitors – do you want to wait for me below on the road, Jo?

Jo Wha'?

Marie Therese (*get lost*) Y'know? I'll meet you after a while. Y'know?

Jo Oh, all right so. See yis.

Jo *exits with bicycle.*

Rabe We've got to get out of here. At once. This place is marked. I like your friend.

Marie Therese Oh she's all right. I have to be careful staying out late meself. Me father, y'know.

Rabe Where can we get petrol? Do you know? It may be a matter of life and death, actually. We're frightfully stuck. No petrol. Rather very little petrol. To go on, I mean.

Marie Therese Oh, is that all you can say to me? Petrol! (*Tears, rushing off.*) Jo! Jo!

Rabe *stands in amazement.* **Jo** *comes back on.*

Rabe I'm afraid your friend – (*Gestures.*) In tears, actually.

Jo Feck it. If she's bawling that's trouble ahoy.

Rabe Stop! Stand there!

Jo Wha'?

Rabe Don't move. Hold that pose. Move your head a little. To the right. Perfect!

Jo Oh Lord, I have this momentous feeling that something is going to happen! It's like being in the pictures.

Rabe It's your profile. No. Head, perhaps? Perfectly sculpted. Rather Italianate. Madonnaesque.

Jo I think I know what you mean and I sincerely hope you don't go on like that any more.

Rabe But you do remind me of someone –

Jo Hope it's not your sister. I'm always reminding boys of their sisters. Know what I mean? (*Rapidly.*) It's kind of like being shunted on to a siding when you'd really like to be going full steam down the main tracks. Stop it, Jo. Keep it simple. Drop the similes.

Rabe I have a confession to make. All that shit just now. Statues, profiles. Simply a technique of mine. I use it with women when I feel I can get away with it. I was trying to attract your attention.

Jo Oh, you attracted my attention okay. No bother.

Rabe (*outburst*) Don't you see what an absolute bastard I am? The way I tried to flatter, to deceive you just now? I don't know why I do it. People say I'm revolting. I am revolting. I have this constant need of petty little conquests. Of course I do enjoy it, sex. I concede that. But where is the deeper basis for it? I believe I may be an emotional monster, stunted, like a dwarf.

Jo (*pause*) Now that we've got that out of the way. Can we go on to something else? Please.

Rabe seizes her and kisses her violently.

Jo (*breaking away*) Mind me glasses! (*She takes off her glasses.*) You can do the same again if you want to.

Rabe What is your secret? You do have a guilty secret, don't you? (**Jo** *puts on her glasses again, slowly.*)

Jo (*very upset*) I didn't mean to harm her, mister. Honest I didn't now.

Rabe Who? What?

Jo The little Lannigan girl they're all looking for. It was me that took her. I just wanted to love her, y'know. I just took her for one night. And then she disappeared again. I'm near frantic with worry – what'll I do?

Rabe My secret. I shall tell you my secret. I lit the flames.

Jo What flames?

Rabe My father's shop. I didn't actually light the fire. Still, I was responsible. I walked all the way home from Liverpool Street. Cross Bishopsgate. Artillery Passage. White's Row. On to Brick Lane. Everywhere they stood about. Watching me. Shaven heads. Black shirts. I passed the Mayfair. I even stopped to see what was on. *Hell's Angels* with Ben Lyon. Have you seen it? Smashing scenes with aeroplanes. Then Blooms Corner. I smelled the fire. Those eyes still watching me. They hate everything that is different, you see.

Jo Who? Who was watching you?

Rabe Blackshirts. Now I keep having these migraines. I would not allow them to mock me. They see me coming. The Blackshirts. They always see me coming. They step in front of me. But I refuse to step aside. I goad them, taunt them! That is why I was responsible for the burning of the shop. Although I wasn't there when they burned it. My father. Do you understand? How one can be responsible while still not there?

Jo I think so.

Rabe (*vehemently*) I hate my father. He just stood there while they burned him out. Why didn't he do something? A figure in a burning sheet. Dancing. (*Great yell.*) Dance, Israelite! Dance.

Jo (*long pause*) Maybe we can do without mothers and fathers, altogether.

Rabe What do you mean? What do you mean by that?

Jo So as we can be ourselves. (*Pause.*) You won't tell on me or anything? Will you? The Sergeant or anyone? About me taking little Nellie Lannigan like that? Sure you won't?

Rabe Course not. Actually, I quite like you.

Jo What do you like most of all? In the whole wide world?

Rabe Oh –

Jo Go on. Say.

Rabe There is danger everywhere. Do you know that? You simply have to touch things and – ping! What I want, more than anything, is a theatre which can hold – danger. You see what I mean? Where danger can detonate upon a stage. You see, I believe if theatre can do that, there will be less – danger left in the world. Our only hope is that art transform the human animal. Nothing else has worked.

Jo (*pause*) I know exactly what you mean.

Rabe Do you really? You? What do you – like?

Jo This very minute? I love the words in geometry.

Rabe I hate mathematics.

Jo So do I. I just love the words. Scalene. Even rectangular. Also rhombus, equilateral, equidistant. Not to mention obtuse, acute, theorem.

Rabe That old queen in there hasn't an earthly idea – she has no conception of what theatre might be –

Jo The woman?

Rabe The man.

Jo Oh.

Rabe I feel completely at ease now. I understand you. You are very precious. Do you know that.

Jo Oh God, this is too much. (*Pause.*) Are you, y'know, a waif?

Rabe I am a victim.

Jo I knew it. We're the same so, you and me. I'm a waif.

Marie Therese (*off*) Jo! Jo-ho! Yoo-hoo!

Rabe Must go – (*He exits rapidly.*)

Jo Oh please don't – feck that one anyways. Just when things were going great guns.

Marie Therese *on with her bicycle. A moment watching* **Jo**.

Marie Therese Well, miss? Where were you?

Jo Waiting for you below on the road as per arrangement.

Marie Therese Oh that man!

Jo What man?

Marie Therese That actor fellow. I've never been so – in all my life.

Jo Wha'?

Marie Therese Promise now, Jo, cross your heart you won't tell –

Jo Won't tell wha'?

Marie Therese Well, he made, y'know, advances at me. I could have died. Still and all he said I was the most beautiful in all the – Y'know. Oh, says I, I bet you say that to your one. What one, says he? The actress one, says I, on the stage. You're the only one, says he, as bold as brass, holding my hand real tight and looking straight into my eyes –

Jo *has begun to exit with her bicycle so that* **Marie Therese** *has to hurry to catch up.*

Marie Therese Jo! Come back here, at once, Jo! I'll never speak to you again, miss. Oh, Jo! Wait!

Lights down. Lights up. Morning light.

The **Sergeant** *leads on* **Lyle Jones**, **Madame MacAdam**, **Sally**, **Rabe** *and* **Simon** *from around the back of the van.*

Lyle Jones A child?

Sergeant Missing, sir. A little girl from the town.

Lyle Jones Perdita!

Sergeant She's one of the Lannigans, sir. A poor family from the Lane.

Madame MacAdam Darling, do let the bobby give the facts.

Lyle Jones These may be good auspices. On the other hand they may be dreadful.

Sergeant Just some routine questions, sir.

Lyle Jones We have nothing to hide. Mere shreds and patches. The actor, my dear man, is forever exposed. You see – contrary to what others may say – I have immense regard for the pluck of actors. Oh my dear sir I could tell you but I shan't of the treachery of others in the business. Madame! Tickets! There we are, Constable! (**Madame** *produces tickets*.)

Sergeant Sergeant, sir.

Lyle Jones On the dot, eight o'clock, nightly. No, no mystery here save the greatest mystery of all – to put on the living vesture of others. Selections from the Bard necessarily abbreviated to suit our modest ensemble. A special repertoire of Celtic plays especially conned for our tour of Eirer. Simon, here is our driver, indispensable with hammer and electricity but the ultimate spear-carrier – darling Simon   –

Sergeant Is that the lot of ye, then, Mr – ah?

Lyle Jones (*bow*) Lyle Jones. Ac-tor manager. My Coriolanus, my Svengali of some little repute in the provinces. I was in the Haymarket in twenty-seven –

Rabe He was up for buggery twice in Bow Street.

Lyle Jones (*stonily*) Ha-ha-ha. Jests among the players, Constable. Idle banter.

Madame MacAdam Darling! Beware the unnecessary barb!

Sergeant Sergeant, sir.

Lyle Jones But of course. Perhaps, Sergeant, you would care to inspect our transport. (*Aside.*) I'll deal with you later, you shitty little –

Rabe *gives him a rude finger and slips off with* **Simon**.

Sergeant Stop!

Rabe Stop me!

Sergeant God Almighty!

Lyle Jones Now, now, Sergeant. I will vouch for both those boys. Absolutely sterling chaps. Not a blemish. Right, everyone?

Sergeant (*towards the van*) What's in here?

Lyle Jones That, sir, contains the banquet of Prospero.

Sergeant I see, bigod.

Sally It's just our props.

Lyle Jones But you and I, Sergeant, we know better, do we not? Look into my eyes. Do you see the ab-yss? I dive nightly into the void. Down! Down! And I – Maybe? Maybe not! – will bring back from these depths the silver branch with delicate leaves, clenched between my teeth.

Sally Can we go now?

Sergeant I'm a bit of a performer myself, you know. The odd recitation.

Lyle Jones Hark! I knew it. A fellow thespian.

Sergeant (*sudden outburst, recitation*)
    T'anam an Dia but there it is!
    The dawn on the hills of Ireland!
    God's Angels lifting the night's black veil
    From the fair, sweet face of my sireland.

Lyle Jones Well-well. Well-well.

Madame MacAdam How very – winning!

Sergeant (*second stanza*)
Oh, Ireland, isn't it grand you look,
Like a bride in her rich adornin'
With all the pent-up love of my heart
I bid you top of the mornin'.

Sally *tries to slip away.*

Sergeant Hold it there, miss. This is an investigation.

Sally Look. This lot came over from Liverpool to Belfast. We crossed the border. Everyone said they loved shows in the Free State. Also plenty of rashers and eggs. I only wish I could get away home again.

Madame MacAdam We came because everywhere else is bedlam.

Sally Now we're stuck. Can you get us some petrol, mister?

Sergeant Sure you shouldn't be travelling the roads at all in the middle of the Emergency.

Lyle Jones Emergency? What emergency?

Sally That's what they call the war down here in the Free State.

Sergeant (*explosion*) 'Course it's an emergency. What else would you call it with the whole country upside down with that carry-on over the water? Isn't Churchill trying to starve us out? And but for the weather we'd have Herr Hitler's bombers in every hayfield in the country. Anyways. It's yer war. If that's so, why aren't ye fighting it?

Madame MacAdam Sir, you mistake us. Do you think we can play in the trenches? Do you think we can perform among the butchers? No. We can only play behind the lines. Beyond is the pit of darkness. (*To* **Sally**.) Come along, dear.

Madame *and* **Sally** *exit.*

Lyle Jones It's one of her better exits, I do assure you.

Sergeant I'm sorry I spoke to her like that, sir.

Lyle Jones Please –

Sergeant Ye're all more than welcome. You know that. It's me nerves. I'll get you the petrol.

Lyle Jones You will! My dear fellow, what can I say? Free tickets for the duration of our stay. Although we may curtail our visit now that we have the petrol –

Sergeant There's a job to be done first –

Lyle Jones A job! What job?

Sergeant Come here a minnit, Mr – ah and I'll put you in the picture.

He leads **Lyle Jones** *off around the van.* **Lyle Jones** *immediately leads* **Madame MacAdam**, **Sally** *and* **Simon** *back on around the other side of the van.*

Madame MacAdam A greyhound?

Lyle Jones I'm afraid so.

Madame MacAdam As in dog? This is preposterous. Am I to lurch from one crisis to another like an ambulance?

Sally If we knew where the petrol is, I'd be game to nick a few gallons. On the QT.

Lyle Jones I'm sure you'd be game, darling, for anything.

Sally Bitch!

Madame MacAdam I shall retire at once from the theatre and do something decent.

Sally No, you won't. You'll always go on.

Madame MacAdam Of course. One must. It simply depends in which direction one chooses to go.

Lyle Jones I shall wear my velour gangster hat from *Winterset* at the dog track. Simon! Wardrobe! The dogman is called – and I tremble at the thought of it – Chamberlain. Imagine our prospects with a name like that!

Madame MacAdam This is not simply immoral, it is inappropriate. Theatre belongs upon a stage, not at the race-track. Otherwise one is in competition with criminals and every conceivable type of uniformed flunkey. (*To* **Lyle Jones**.) Have you forgotten what happened with that landlady in Bradford?

Lyle Jones Not my fault that she uncovered our little stratagem.

Madame MacAdam We shall never be able to play Bradford again.

Lyle Jones Nonsense. Bradford awaits us with bated breath. Come along, Simon.

Exits with **Simon**.

Madame MacAdam Although my perceptions are crystal clear I seem utterly unable to influence what is about to happen. I simply dread these charades among the natives.

Sally So what, if he brings it off? It may get us out of this hole.

Madame MacAdam (*towards the absent* **Lyle Jones**) Can you
believe that I was once besotted with that man! I was originally
married to a solicitor Mr Twine of Worcester when I first met
Lyle Jones. He – I mean Lyle Jones – came out of the Welsh
valleys like a visitation upon those of us who lived east of the
Severn. I pursued him from Bristol to Cardiff. I believed that
if he did not take me away with him, I would be doomed
for life, living with Mr Twine. He, I mean Lyle Jones, had
a kind of beauty in everything that he did. Was it merely
being younger? In those days he would take the most dreadful
rubbish and transform it upon the stage. I did not know then
what I know now, that he is utterly incapable of discrimination
of any kind. Once there is a flicker of an audience he begins
to perform. Can it be that the very source of our art is also
the source of our decline? Can one destroy a talent by grossly
overusing it?

Sally Why don't you leave him so? I would in your boots.

Madame MacAdam What a question! My dear, he and I
have given ourselves to one another. In our fashion.

Sally If it's over you cut your losses. Get out. The thing is
to know when that happens. Anyhow. Acting. It's no big
deal. You do it, you don't do it. You do it good, you make
a dog's dinner of it. Just go and do it and be done with it.
What's the fuss? That's what I say to Rabe. He gets mad
at me then. Starts yelling at me. Know something? Times I
don't know what you lot go on about. As God is my judge
I don't.

Madame MacAdam Actually, Mr Twine was very decent
about it. He allowed me to take what remained of my
trousseau. Together with one or two items from the mantelpiece.
Unbeknownst to him I had substantial savings in the British
Midlands and Colonial. We women must always be prepared
for the quick getaway.

Sally Don't I know it. I never unpack fully, myself.

Madame MacAdam How shall I describe my departure from the banks of the Severn except to say that more than ever I looked upon that river as a great sluice, a great cut into the heart of England. It was immediately after that other war and melancholia was rife. So I did the only sensible thing. I took to the roads with Lyle Jones. And now I have dwindled to petty criminality among the Irish.

Re-enter **Simon** *and* **Lyle Jones**. **Lyle Jones** *is now dressed in a long flowing black coat and wide-brimmed hat.*

Lyle Jones (*with a twirl*) Well, darlings, what do you think? Dog people are absolutely marvellous dressers, you know. Simon, let us find ourselves a dog! (*Off.*)

Blackout.

Scene Three

Music. Projection: **Two Full Confessions. A Shakespearean Interlude. A Heart is broken. And there is a brief vision of Hell.**

Marie Therese *and* **Jo** *are sitting at the kitchen table of the* **Sergeant**'*s house, supposedly doing their homework.*

Marie Therese And you stole her?

Jo I didn't steal her.

Marie Therese But you took her?

Jo I only took her to a safe place. Just to make her – happy.

Marie Therese Where?

Jo Our shed out the back at me Auntie's house.

Marie Therese And now she's gone again?

Jo Yeh.

Marie Therese You're going to go to jail, so y'are.

Jo You promised not to tell!

Marie Therese I have to tell me diary.

Jo It's all right to tell your diary. But not another soul, now.

Marie Therese It's so exciting, so it is! What're ya going to do now, Jo?

Jo I don't care about anything any more, so I don't. I think we might be in for a bit of an apocalypse.

Marie Therese A bit of a wha'?

The **Sergeant** *has come in and the two girls begin to do their homework, furiously. He, meantime, walks about, peering over their shoulders, whistling 'Roses of Picardy' through his teeth.*

Marie Therese For the Lord's sake Daddy stop that whistlin'. We have oceans of homework to do, don't we Jo?

Sergeant What age are you now, Jo?

Jo I'm going on seventeen, Sergeant.

Marie Therese Ah, Daddy, she's two months younger than me and well you know it. What's gotten into him!

Sergeant I was thinking, Jo, we might have a chat.

Marie Therese It's always the same so it is. No-one pays a whit of attention to anything I ever say.

Sergeant Take this young fella now that's acting in the plays beyond.

Marie Therese Oh God now we're done for!

Jo His name is Rabe. He showed me where they bet him. He has scars everywhere. On his arms and legs and body everywhere. He said he's always been separate all his life. I said me too. He said he's acting on the stage only to find the lost person in himself. (*Slowly.*) He said he has to keep trying all the time to start all over again. (*Pause.*) I said me too.

Marie Therese (*pause. Hiss*) You were talkin' to him so ya were! 'N you were supposed to be my best friend! Behind me back. Oh!

Sergeant Stop! The two of ye. Now what I want to know is this and no beating about the bush. Has he ever laid a hand on either of the two of ye? Your man?

Marie Therese (*jump. Scream*) Daddy! Such a question to ask!

A loud banging overhead. All three look up.

Sergeant There! Look at that! You've got your mother off again. Will ya go up to her in the name of God.

Marie Therese (*tears*) Oh, Mammy.

She rushes off. **Jo** *begins to gather up her school-books and school-bag.*

Jo Sergeant, if you were to be locked up in jail, y'know, I mean would they let you have books to read whenever you wanted?

Sergeant It's the curse of Adam. One minute bombing with aeroplanes, the next minute entertaining up on stage, one minute having a kind conversation with your own kith and kin, the next minute roaring and fighting like tinkers. There's a crack down the middle of the human specimen and no doubt about it.

Jo Jail, Sergeant.

Sergeant Jail? Jail what?

Jo Me.

Sergeant You? Will you stop your raving, girl, and go on home with you. No-one's going to harm you, I'll see to that I promise you. (*Afterthought.*) Bloody actors.

Jo I just have to follow things through. To the bitter end. You know what I mean, Sergeant? It's like my – apotheosis. You know?

The **Sergeant** *stands watching her walk off. Lights down.*

Lights up on the van. **Madame MacAdam** *sweeps on followed by* **Rabe**.

Rabe You're disappointed in me. Yet again.

Madame MacAdam Darling. Do try to rid yourself of this self-pity. It is terribly enervating for all those about you.

Rabe You said –

Madame MacAdam I said you had insulted Lyle. Which you have. He is frightfully hurt.

Rabe I cannot tolerate shit.

Madame MacAdam Perhaps you should try to tolerate – as you elegantly put it – shit.

Rabe How can you? You of all people! Say such a – defending the second-rate!

Madame MacAdam Second-rate! First-rate! That is the language of the race-track.

Rabe Where is it, then? The glorious miracle of theatre that you talked about?

Madame MacAdam I do believe you are looking for religion. A mistake, I'm afraid. For Heaven's sake, do you think the miracle of theatre is found beneath trapdoors and behind dry ice? Rubbish. It is built upon acceptance –

Rabe Acceptance?!

Madame MacAdam It is built upon human error and human frailty and, yes, what you so dismissively describe as the second-rate. It is built upon patience with what actually exists. Not some cloud-cuckoo-land. If we bear witness to the steady pulse of the world there is no miracle which we may not accomplish upon the stage.

Rabe I came to you to try to find some meaning that I could –

Madame MacAdam You came, if I remember correctly, to our doorstep in East Putney in answer to an ad for an experienced juvenile. In conversations like this one, exact statistics are important. Actually you looked more like a battered, Dickensian orphan. Do please remember where we started from. Otherwise we will get nowhere.

Rabe But why are you putting on rubbish to entertain a lot of yokels? Don't you see how demeaning it is? Don't you see how it infects everyone who touches it?

Madame MacAdam Oh, dear, you are so very young.

Rabe (*explosion*) There you go! Patronizing me. You're doing exactly the same thing as Lyle. I am not an invalid. What I'm trying to effect is to create some kind of standard while you lot have thrown everything away.

Madame MacAdam You may well be right. One's standards are, or at least ought to be, in direct relation to one's talents. We are not greatly talented, alas, merely dedicated. And sometimes inspired.

Rabe Are you suggesting that I have no talent?

Madame MacAdam On the contrary. I think you may be very talented.

Rabe Really? Do you think so? Your saying that means everything to me. You know, sometimes I feel that I'm an utter, utter failure. But for Sally in there I would have done away with myself.

Madame MacAdam What? When was this?

Rabe It doesn't matter.

Madame MacAdam Sally never mentioned this to me.

Rabe Sally is very strong.

Madame MacAdam I do not doubt her strength. It's her safety that I worry about.

Rabe Please. I'm going to pull myself together. I really am. I simply must be taken seriously. That is all.

Madame MacAdam Have you ever doubted me?

Rabe You are the only person that I have never doubted. You make me feel, somehow, a whole person and not this silly get who causes distress to people. I should hate to ever cause you distress. You know that. I draw this immense courage from your strength. Just let me be close to you, to be tender with you, simply to touch you –

Madame MacAdam Oh dear.

Rabe I will also try to make it up to Lyle.

Madame MacAdam Now that does please me.

Rabe Will you let me kiss you?

Madame MacAdam Certainly not. I need to take a walk. Alone.

Rabe It would help if I didn't have to watch him act. Otherwise the old sod is pretty decent.

Madame MacAdam There is a great deal that you might learn from watching him act.

Rabe Oh? Like what?

Madame MacAdam Playfulness. (*Departing in haste.*) I really must get some air. My palpitations. (*She sweeps off around the van.*)

Rabe What's that all about, then? Bloody women!

Sally (*entering quickly*) What's up? Madame said you needed me.

Rabe She did, did she? That what she said? What a lark!

Sally (*turning off again*) OK – OK. That's fine with me. Bye-bye, lover.

Rabe (*stopping her*) No, Sally, please. Didn't mean that. Really. What I mean is – well. What else did she say? I mean Madame. About me?

Sally Look. I don't know what this game's all about but it's bloody boring, that's what.

Rabe I've got to ask you something. You're the only one who understands. Do you think I've begun to crack up again? Do you?

Sally Here we go again. There's bugger-all wrong with you, mate. Maybe self-indulgence, to be sure. Yes.

Rabe You see it's as if I keep throwing myself against those walls. You remember? I told you about it. That room. Always the same room. When they closed that door on me it was always the same room even though they must have locked me into many different rooms over all those years –

Sally (*warning*) Rabe –

Rabe Walls are always the same. Some are of brick, some whitewashed, some padded.

Sally (*outburst*) I'm not going to let you do this, you hear? I'm not letting you back into that again! That was years ago! That's all over!

Rabe (*genuine surprise*) What're you talking about, love?

Sally (*examining him*) Are you having me on? That's it, isn't it? Just trying to frighten me you are. Another of your crazy games. Another big performance.

Rabe Don't know what you're on about, love.

Sally You were back in that bloody awful fucking hospital again, that's what. Raving you were about being locked up again.

Rabe (*perfectly normal explanation*) Oh. I see. It's just my shoulder.

Sally Your what?

Rabe My shoulder. See! All down there. Tender to the touch. It's been like that for days now. Bruised. Black and blue. I can't sleep on it. Just like when I used to throw myself against those walls.

Sally (*embracing him, holding him*) Oh, Rabe, please don't do this to yourself, please –

Rabe What I want, see, is to make this happen upon a stage. Curtain goes up, a man's skull opens up and we see the inside. All these creatures parade and dance. Such costumes, you've never seen the like, raging colours, material like metal and fur, all pouring out of this skull. Then it all ends, this play or whatever, this play ends in a great red hunt. The hunting down of these creatures, actors carrying long, pointed spears, see. And sound, yes, drums but also strange instruments like horns or bugles but different, whistles and conches. It's a moving painting right now, in my head. I want to play the hunter and the hunted at the same time. You know what I mean?

Sally Why don't you let me near you?

Rabe But you're incredibly near to me.

Sally It hurts when you say that. You know that? Really hurts.

Rabe But you're the very last person I should wish to hurt.

Sally You never let anyone near you, ever. Whenever anyone tries you skip off somewhere else. Somewhere in your head. I know I don't understand all these things. But when I give myself to something I give myself to it until it's all gone. Are you all gone, Rabe? Makebelieve, God, I can't stand makebelieve. It's what causes all the trouble. I really believe that, I do.

Rabe What did she mean, Madame? What was she talking about? I have nothing to learn from that old fruit Lyle. Nothing!

Sally Do you listen to a word I say?

Rabe I'm going to blast him off the stage!

Sally Poor old Lyle.

Rabe Poor old Lyle blocks everything we, you and I, should be doing with ourselves. We shouldn't *be* here. We should be on some great stage together playing the great parts. You and I could create great power together. And, yes I do listen to everything you say and I love you – (**Sally** *has begun to move off again.*) What is it?

Sally Self-preservation maybe. Maybe I'll go find Madame. Maybe we can hold hands together. (*Exits.*)

Rabe Madame. Yes. What did she mean? His playfulness? (*Shift: head back, great vigour.*) I will be the hunter and the hunted! I will be the knife and the wound! I will be the spear and the quivering flesh! (*Sudden shift again: down to puzzlement.*) What could she have meant? Playfulness?

Lights down on **Rabe**.

The side of the van opens. **Lyle Jones**, *in his crombie coat and velour hat with the greyhound on a leash.* **Slipper** *stands to one side as his 'audience'.*

Lyle Jones (*to* **Slipper**) The dog? My dear boy, I positively adore the dog. The dog is dearer to me than homo sap. Do you know, by the bye, why most actors dislike the dog? No? Competition. Are you familiar, perhaps, with *The Shaughraun*? No? Never mind. Best thing in it, the dog. Put a dog upon the stage and oh my God what a natural! Perhaps, dear, you have wondered down the years as you frequented this playhouse and that why it is that bitchery is rampant behind the footlights? Hm? Wonder no more. (*Hand up.*) Please! Don't ask. I know precisely what is in your mind. I can see the very question forming this instant upon your brow. Why? Why, you ask, why does the dog not threaten Lyle Jones? Hm? A most commendable question. A very contingent question. Indeed. Well. I shall tell you, darling. (*Whisper.*) Eye-contact. I reduce the dog, thus. (*Bends, looks into the greyhound's eyes.* **Slipper** *bends and does likewise.*) Thereafter the dog knows his place upon the stage. Allow me to illustrate. (*Removes coat and hat, handing them over to* **Slipper**.) Stand off a pace! You are familiar with *Two Gentlemen*? No? Never mind. Not one of the Bard's better efforts I do concede but Launce! Divine Launce and his dog Crab! Observe clearly. (*Immediately in part with the greyhound, as* Crab.) 'Nay, I'll be sworn, I have sat in the stocks for puddings he has stolen, otherwise he hath been executed; I have stood on the pillory for geese he hath killed, otherwise he hath suffered for't. (*To greyhound.*) Thou thinkest not of this now. Nay, I remember the trick you served me when I took my leave of Madame Silvia. Did I not bid thee still mark me and do as I do? When didst thou see me heave my leg and make water against a gentlewoman's farthingale? Didst thou ever see me do such a trick?' (*Pause. To* **Slipper**.) Well? What is your considered view? You see! The dog is absolutely beneath my control. My dear boy, you mustn't fret. We shall simply slay them at the dog track. Slay them!

Slipper *looks at him, mouth open. Lights down. Sides of the van close.*

Lights up: night light. **Madame MacAdam**, *followed by a weary* **Sally**, *has climbed up a hill over the town.*

Madame MacAdam Are we on the highest point?

Sally Yes.

Madame MacAdam I must be able to see clearly in each direction if I am to regain my equanimity. I need to replenish and tone my bodily spirits.

Sally We can't go any higher than this.

Madame MacAdam He has defiled his art by mingling with that racing animal. Has he brought down upon us the curse of failure?

Sally He's only trying to con a few gallons of petrol.

Madame MacAdam I am not referring to deception. There is always an element of deception in theatre. We create through concealment. That is why absolute shits are capable of creating great beauty upon the stage. No! I am not talking about deceit. I am talking about triviality. If one must perform, one must perform with the greatest risk. Rabe does.

Sally (*pause. Slowly*) I love Rabe.

Madame MacAdam I am afraid that he may destroy you.

Sally Yes. (*Pause.*) I know.

Madame MacAdam At this point I should say something like: Do be careful. Try to discriminate between the different roles which he plays for you.

Sally I don't know what you're on about. He's always Rabe to me.

Madame MacAdam Remarkable! Women. Truly remarkable. The way they put up with male destructiveness.

Sally I like the way he shifts about. I like the way you never know with him. I've had me fill in me time of the other sort. Where I come from the men are all full of bibles and silence and cocoa. I like the way Rabe is always changing. It's like colour.

Madame MacAdam You're not under the illusion, are you, that you can save him? Or some such rot?

Sally I can try and protect him from the worst of it.

Madame MacAdam I'm afraid he may not want that.

Sally So be it.

Madame MacAdam Forgive me for asking but aren't you a little, shall we say, unnerved by his promiscuity?

Sally Why should I be?

Madame MacAdam Why, he has even made overtures towards me!

Sally (*laugh*) And didn't you like it?

Madame MacAdam I confess I found it a trifle – steamy.

Sally What you said just now. About not being – trivial. That's it, isn't it? That's all that counts. I mean between Rabe and me. It's not – trivial.

Madame MacAdam At my age – no, no, I mustn't ever use that phrase again. It's simply hiding behind a ludicrous visage. Why, he made me feel young! Young! I admit it. It was absolutely exhilarating!

Sally Wonderful! That's just wonderful.

Madame MacAdam Throw the proverbial caution to the winds! Do not retreat! Forward, forward! Good heavens, I do sound like one of those dreadful military types, don't I?

Sally That's right! No retreat!

Madame MacAdam Into the breach!

Sally Over the top!

Madame MacAdam (*hand to heart*) Oh, dear, this is too much – I really must calm down! It must have something to do with being marooned in this place. I wonder if we are actually in retreat from the war?

Sally Do you think we are?

Madame MacAdam Don't know. Did think we were trying to keep the spirits up. But why here? The Irish are absolutely insulated against any outside incursion. They are utterly immune to reality.

Sally They said in Belfast this would be like a foreign country. It has nothing to do with distance, they said. It may be only a hundred miles, they said but you'll feel it's a thousand. Red Indians, they said. They're like bloody Red Indians down there. They don't like Red Indians in Belfast. Me? I always wanted to see the Red Indians for myself.

Madame MacAdam (*deep breathing*) I begin, finally, to feel an inhalation, an opening of the pores.

Sally I want to go home.

Madame MacAdam Do you think he might have molested the missing child?

Sally Who? Rabe?

Madame MacAdam Lyle Jones.

Sally Never.

Madame MacAdam He is undersexed. Men who are undersexed are given to experiment. The same, unfortunately, is true of men who are oversexed.

Sally I never think about such things with people I know. I always think the real horrors are somewhere else. I haven't a titer of wit, do you know that? (*Pause.*) I must tell you, though. The Irish can be wicked dangerous when it comes down to one of their own.

Madame MacAdam This is an extremely dangerous country. How can you perform theatre before a population of performers? They constantly complete one's lines for one. Frequently with improvisations of a local character. They constantly interrupt with advice and criticism and directions as to one's posture. It is intolerable. More. It is a violation of one's function. The Irish have no tact. I will confine our tours in future to the Home Counties and one or two selected venues north of Coventry.

Sally Just look at those lights!

Madame MacAdam To keep at bay the principle of chaos. That is what is urgent. To deny the one with cloven feet.

Sally Just look at it. Lit up. No wonder the Jerries can bomb Belfast.

Madame MacAdam Look, my dear, but remember the darkness beyond.

Lights down.

Lights up: a drunken **Bun Bourke** *in baker's whites before the van.*

Bourke (*towards van*) And what about the little Lannigan girl? Hah? Oho! Where is she so? Question. I'm going to report you, boy. Question. Who made the world? No answer. Ha? Fucking atheists. Pure people don't carry on, putting on the act, trying to be what they're not. (*Suddenly banging his fists on the side of the van.*) Come outa there! Infiltrators! Come out and show your born faces, will ye! Paint and powder, mincy-mancy, shaping and dressing and stripping and putting on the act. People like fools sitting on forms, watching, giggling and gawking, sucking sweets, clapping and roaring. Hidden places merging into daylight. Turn off, turn on, night when it's day, day when it's night –

He staggers off with a kind of sob. Side of the van opens. The stage with front curtain closed. **Rabe** *and* **Jo**, *clutching one another, are lying naked on a makeshift bed.*

Jo 'S all right. He's gone.

Rabe What did he mean? What did he mean?

Jo He's soft in the head. You don't have to worry about it –

Rabe Feel my chest. There. The pounding has started again. It's as if it will burst.

Jo *kisses him on the chest.*

Jo I've never kissed anyone's skin before. Is there a word for hard and soft at the same time?

She puts on her spectacles and he takes them off again.

Rabe You keep putting these back on –

Jo I'm blind as a bat without them –

Rabe But your eyes are extraordinarily beautiful.

Jo You can go in and out of me again. If you want to. Do you want to?

Rabe There is so very little time left to us.

Jo So what?

Rabe Afterwards –

Jo Afterwards is for tomorrow. Oh Lord, I know I shouldn't feel, y'know, euphoric. 'Tis bad luck. Something awful always happens whenever I feel euphoric. If they were to open up the curtain there now we could perform for all and sundry. Couldn't you see their faces! I suppose you think I'm y'know, impetuous. Oh God, Jo, shut up and stop babbling.

Rabe We are always performing. Only the audience changes.

Jo (*cry*) That's not true. I know the difference.

Rabe I'm sorry. I didn't wish to upset you.

Jo I could go off with you.

Rabe No, no, no, no. I mean I should like you to. But I will never subject you to – all that.

Jo It's not makebelieve, is it?

Rabe But you were so brave a moment ago.

Jo Just lie on top of me again. If you were to lie on top of me I could feel all of you like before. Then I could believe it is true.

He embraces her and they begin to make love. Lights down.

Lights up on **Marie Therese** *in her nightdress in bed, writing in her diary.*

Marie Therese He begged me and begged me but I said no, never. He was so insistent. (*Spelling.*) I–n–c. No. He was – mad at me. It is my honour, I said. Your hair is lovely tonight, he said. I had to give in to him. I couldn't help myself. (*Head up. Not writing.*) Everywan says I'm good-looking. Well, why don't things ever work out for me, so? (*Writing again.*) I will never speak to J again. She is a B. I will find a new best friend maybe Mary Murphy though she is an awful swank. (*Stops.*) God I could murder that other one so I could if I could only get my hands on her.

Lights down.

Lights back on **Jo** *and* **Rabe**. *There is the sound of marching feet, distant, now nearer, suddenly very loud, then cut off.*

Rabe (*leaping up*) Did you hear that?

Jo It's nothing. Come back to me, please –

Rabe Sounds of feet –

Jo I heard nothing –

Rabe Don't touch me. I'm sorry. I should never have brought you into this –

Jo It's what I want. I wanted – if we could just hold on to each other it'd be all right. I know it.

Rabe (*pointing*) Look!

Jo It's nothing – there's nothing there –

Rabe (*scream*) Look! Can you not see!

He stands pointing back.

Jo There's nothing there. Please. It's only me. Jo.

Across the back in silhouette, the figures of **Bun Bourke** *and his* **LDF Men** *but now in Nazi uniforms.*

Lights down.

Part Two

Scene Four

Music. Projection: **The lovers are apprehended! The Death of Hamlet. The River is dragged and a Messenger arrives.**

Night light.

Kerosene lamps out of the darkness. **Bun Bourke** *and his* **LDF Men** *in uniform pushing the naked figures of* **Rabe** *and* **Jo** *forward into the light.* **Jo** *is screaming and the men are roaring.*

Bourke Halt! Nice! I must say – nice. Lookit them. Will ya for Jasus' sake lookit them! Naked whores. Up on her. Prick.

Jo Leave him alone, leave him alone!

Bourke Go on home you filthy little bitch before I fucking break your – (*Directions.*) Stop! Release her, men. Let her go. But hauld onto him. Tighter. Tight! The prime boy. Aha, you rover, you.

1st LDF Man (*to* **Jo**) Go on home miss like he says. Go on and get your clothes and go home out of this.

2nd LDF Man Bate the fuckin' face offa her.

1st LDF Man Leave her alone now.

Bourke C'mon, c'mon, c'mon with yis. Down to the Town Hall with him! Tight hold. Slippery tit. I'll get it out of him if it's the last thing I do before I fucking drop. I'll make him talk, boy.

Jo What're you going to do to him? Please?

1st LDF Man Little Lannigan girl.

2nd LDF Man She's missing.

3rd LDF Man Maybe murdered by your man.

Jo No!

Bourke No talk with civilians, men. No consorting. Quick march. Creeping in here with their contraptions.

Jo He didn't do anything. It was me that did it. Me!

Rabe Maybe the child has to die. A necessary sacrifice.

Bourke Hear him? Did ye all? By Jasus I'll melt him, the ram. I'll fucking melt him.

Jo Can't you listen, any of you?

Rabe Now I know what it is! To be the knife and the wound. To be the killer and the dead child.

Jo Rabe! No! Don't say that! You're only killing yourself! Your father, Rabe! Remember your father!

Bourke Did ye all record that, men? Did ye? The buck recites. Mark his recitation. And not a hand on him. Lift the fucker out of here before I lose me senses. C'mon, c'mon –

Rabe *is hauled away.* **Jo** *is left alone. She enters the van and it opens up, lit as before: the stage with the stage-curtain closed. She roots about in the makeshift bed. She finds* **Rabe***'s clothes and momentarily clutches them to her. She begins to dress herself, in tears. The sound of a child weeping in the distance.* **Jo** *stops and listens. Sides of the van close.*

Lights down. Lights up: day light. **Madame MacAdam** *and* **Sally** *stand looking off as at a distant spectacle.* **Marie Therese** *is crouched at their feet, not daring to look.*

Lyle Jones *sweeps on with* **Simon**. *No-one pays the slightest attention to him.*

Lyle Jones Darlings! I've got it! Chin up everyone! I've solved our problem. We shall play the abbreviated version of the Death of Hamlet. Madame in trousers as King, Sally as Queen, Simon as a mute Osric. But spoken to. Cut, cut. Perhaps these children could be dressed as courtiers? The boy Rabe, if he can be found, as Laertes. And I, as Prince. (*Pause.*) Do you think the policeman could be schooled as Horatio? No lines, of course. Except now cracks a noble heart. Cut, cut down to good night sweet prince etcetera. Curtain. We can dispense with the dead march. Always thought it unnecessary. What is essential is the duel. And Hamlet, of course. What do you think, darlings? Must do something. Haven't been on stage for a week. Terribly demoralizing. Morale of company. What do you say? (*No answer.*) Very well. I can see I have been utterly abandoned. I shall take my talents elsewhere.

Madame MacAdam Lyle Jones! Why are you doing this?

Lyle Jones Why? Because I am second-rate. That's why. Haven't you heard? Second-rate. Come along, Simon.

He sweeps off again.

Madame MacAdam Second-rate? Second-rate? He never uses such vulgar language. What on earth is the matter with him? Something peculiar is afoot. Hamlet, indeed! We are incapable of mustering a company to perform a sing-song. And now I'm beginning to see theatre everywhere about me. Is this illumination or simply the beginnings of dementia?

Sally (*pointing off*) Look! I think they're starting back!

Madame MacAdam Lyle Jones is about to give a celebrity performance at a race-track. And now the policeman is down there with his cohort on the riverbank performing some archaic ritual with grappling-irons.

Marie Therese Oh how could anyone go through life with a father the like of that. He'll be drownded so he will and he can't swim a stroke! Does anywan know what I've to put up with?

Enter **Jo**, *who sits to one side.*

Sally Is the river deep down there?

Marie Therese That's Powlshawn. It's a swally-hole. Isn't it, Jo? Everything in the town always ends up down there. They drag it when a body's missing. Don't tell me! Did they find the child's body yet?

Jo (*jump*) Oh please no –

Sally Their hands are empty.

Marie Therese Oh he's always trying to be the big fella, me father, and he's not a big fella at all!

Madame MacAdam Men must go through the motions, dear. Be thankful when it is only flim-flam. When their full energies are engaged they can be murderous.

Sally You're frightening the two wee girls.

Madame MacAdam I am frightening myself.

Lyle Jones *crosses behind in his crombie and velour hat, followed by* **Slipper** *with the greyhound. He avoids the women but not before* **Madame** *sees him. He,* **Slipper** *and the greyhound scamper into the van.*

Madame MacAdam Lyle Jones! What is the use? I do believe we are stuck in the Land of Nod. Do you realise there may be no resolution? No victory for the animal in this wretched dog race? No laurels, in short no petrol. The townspeople treat us like refugees. Are we to be imprisoned in this place for the duration of the war relying upon the most intricate black market this side of Istanbul?

Sally I'll walk to Belfast first.

*The **Sergeant** enters carrying coils of steel rope and hooks over his shoulders. He is very wet.*

Sergeant We got nowhere fast, I'm telling you. We'll never find the little wan now.

Marie Therese Oh, Daddy, stop. You were great so you were out on the water. Wasn't he, everywan?

Sergeant I'm finished, child. They'll have my stripes for this, I'm telling you. I'll be transferred to the back of beyond.

Marie Therese Oh, Daddy, cheer up!

Sally You did your best.

Madame MacAdam Courage, Sergeant, courage. We are all under the same cloud of periodic failure clearing to periodic success.

Sergeant Is it clouds? Looking at them clouds. I ask meself. Is that all there is to it? Also the body ageing daily without let-up. Nature won't hide anything from us. She's gone, the misfortunate child. But when the time is ripe her remains will turn up. Excuse me, ladies, for talking this way. It was looking into that black hole of water below that did it to me. Aren't we carried everywhere be the flow? Isn't the ground we stand on only resting on water?

Marie Therese Get a grip on yourself, Daddy. What're the neighbours going to think of us?

Sergeant All right, so. It was being over the water that did it to me. Now that I'm on terra firma I'll be all right. Quaking like a jelly, I was.

*A cry off: 'Sergeant! Sergeant!' Enter **Young Maher**, running.*

Young Maher You're wanted, Sergeant.

Sergeant They've arrived to get me. I'll hand in the uniform forthwith.

Madame MacAdam What is it? Speak up!

Young Maher They have the amusement man captured.

Sergeant What amusement man?

Young Maher The young fella.

Madame MacAdam Who? What is this?

Young Maher Bun and the lads. They bet the confession out of him. He killed the little Lannigan girl, he says. They want him sentenced. Bun said to send for the hangman beyond in England, Mr Pierpoint to come and hang him.

Sergeant God give me patience with the lot of ye.

Sally Rabe!

Madame MacAdam Sergeant, you must do something!

Sergeant That boy's no murderer and that gobdaw Bourke will be the death of me yet.

Sally Is it our Rabe?

Young Maher That's his name. (*Pointing at* **Jo**.) He was caught riding that young wan. The two of them were at it without a stitch of clothes on either of them. Riding her he was.

Madame MacAdam This has to be stopped! We must act! Now!

Everyone looks at **Jo**.

Marie Therese Oh you hussy-you! Mammy, Mammy –

She rushes off, in tears.

Jo (*slowly*) 'Twas I took the little Lannigan girl. She was so unhappy, always crying and with no-one to care for her. I took her where she could be happy. But then she disappeared on me. I don't care what happens to me now.

Sergeant (*outrage, to* **Young Maher**) Will you look at what you've done, you ignorant galoot talking like that in front of females!

Young Maher I'm only telling.

Sergeant I'm only telling. All you're capable of telling is lies of the first order. Here with you! Go on! You're coming with me, mister, down to that other gang of lootheramawns –

Sergeant *marches off with* **Young Maher**.

Madame MacAdam (*to* **Sally**) Go with them and fetch the boy. I will wait here for Lyle Jones.

Sally *goes to* **Jo**.

Sally (*to* **Jo**) Just don't let them get to you. OK? They'll try everything to break you. Don't let them. OK?

Sally *goes off*.

Jo Who does that wan think she is, anyways? I was telling the truth so I was. 'Twas I took little Nellie Lannigan. 'Twas I caused everything.

Madame MacAdam (*to* **Jo**) I'm afraid no-one believes you, my dear. It is quite extraordinary how one is so seldom believed when one speaks the truth. On the other hand people have an endless capacity to accept the most outrageous fabrications. Are you all right, dear?

Jo Why did she go off to find Rabe? The actress one just now. Is it that they're lovers?

Madame MacAdam Yes. (*Pause.*) I'm afraid, dear, he is entirely promiscuous. You should know that, shouldn't you?

Jo Yes.

Madame McAdam It's not that he would be uncaring of you. I could see the devotion he would give you. But Rabe is one of those boys who bestows absolute attention on what is immediately in front of him. Until it is replaced by something else. For this reason he is a superb actor. He also believes the gothic hordes are in pursuit of him.

Jo I believed everything he told me.

Madame MacAdam And so did he, I'll be bound. He may have been acting a great part and believing every moment of it. That is Rabe, I'm afraid.

Jo So he was only pretending to me?

Madame MacAdam I'm afraid he may look on life as just a larger stage with a larger audience. Not wise. No, we must never confuse theatre and everyday life. What is proper in one is inappropriate in the other. Are you sure you are all right, dear?

Jo I could face anything now. I mean I could face my nemesis, if I had to.

Madame MacAdam Well, let's hope it doesn't come to that. One should be cautious about rousing the gods especially when one has given oneself to love.

Lights down.

Scene Five

Music. Projection: **A friendship is tested. The Return of Rabe. Madame MacAdam on the subject of Harmony. And the Great Stage of Fools.**

Lights up. The two girls enter with their bicycles.

Marie Therese Why aren't you wearing your glasses any more?

Jo Because.

Marie Therese You'll run into someone on the bike. (*Spiteful.*) Four eyes!

Jo I may have to go off.

Marie Therese Off where?

Jo Maybe Central America. The Balkans is out of the question with the war on.

Marie Therese Ah go on. You're only mad because of them awful things young Maher said about you in front of everyone. You must have died. I'd have died if anywan said such.

Jo They're true.

Marie Therese They're what true?

Jo True. Rabe and me were lovers in that van beyond.

Marie Therese You're a bare-faced liar so you are!

Jo (*fierce shout*) We're lovers! We're lovers! We're lovers!

Marie Therese You're ravin'! It's me he fancies. (*Anger.*) Squinty-face!

Jo We did it together.

Marie Therese Did what together? Is it kissing? I don't want to hear another word of it. I'm not listening.

Jo I thought I'd be afraid. But I wasn't. It just happened so easy. He's so strong. I never knew a boy could be so strong. It was like being there and also being somewhere else. I just can't get over it.

Marie Therese You're just trying to make me cry, you mean strap! (*Tears.*) I'm not going to cry so I'm not.

Jo He put it into me. Y'know? His thing. He put it into my, well, aperture.

Marie Therese He put what into your what? What are ya talking about?

Jo Y'know. The number one place. (*Pointing to her crotch.*) There.

Marie Therese (*outburst*) You you filthy thing to say such a thing! Now I'm going to have to confess it in confession along with yourself –

Jo It's not a bit filthy. That's what I wanted to tell you, Marie Therese. It is lovely. The most lovely thing you could think of –

Marie Therese (*tears. Hurt. Frightened*) Filthy, filthy, filthy –

Jo I'd go to the ends of the earth with him if he wanted me to –

Marie Therese Making up lies, so you are, just to torment me –

Jo I'm not!

Marie Therese You are!

Jo I'm not!

Marie Therese You are! You are! You are! You're nothing but a brazen hussy and Mammy always said you were.

Jo All right so.

Marie Therese Anyways they're locking that fella up so they are. Daddy's going to arrest him.

Jo There's nothing to arrest him for –

Marie Therese God that crowd! There's been nothing but trouble from day one since that amusement crowd came here!

Jo That's not true. We make our own trouble.

Marie Therese (*shift*) I'm getting a new dress adin in the Monster House in Kilkenny polka dots with a chinee collar and an alice bow at the back twenty-nine and eleven.

Jo That's nice.

Marie Therese (*tears*) I'm not going to have any best friend if you're not my best friend any more.

Jo I'll be your best friend.

Marie Therese Honest?

Jo Honest.

Marie Therese Me Mammy never said that about you being a brazen hussy. I just made it up. Forgive and forget, Jo? Please?

Jo Forgive and forget, so.

Pause.

Jo Marie Therese. When you think about, y'know, boys do you think about boys or do you think about stories about boys?

Marie Therese I don't let meself have immodest thoughts if that's what you mean, miss.

Jo There's a terrible difference. I love stories but stories are only stories. You can't touch people in stories. Do you ever talk to your Mammy and Daddy?

Marie Therese Sure I talk to them day and night.

Jo No, I mean talk, really talk. About things. Things that make you anxious?

Marie Therese Course not. Such a notion!

Jo There are times when I feel I don't have a mother and father at all even though they're beyond in England. (*Puts on glasses.*) Right. Are we off so?

Jo *departs off.*

Marie Therese (*following*) Jo, wait! It'll be all right, won't it? It'll all be the same as before? Jo? Did you really just make it all up? About your man? Did you, Jo?

They have gone off. A noise like distant heavy gun-fire. **Rabe**, *dishevelled, beaten, is helped on by* **Sally**.

Rabe There is always, isn't there, a room waiting? Waiting for a town meeting, perhaps. Or a local court. Because up above there was this bloody big ornate bench, carved wood, the lot. For a magistrate, maybe. Or some sort of big-wig.

Sally Forget about it.

Rabe They stood me up in front of him and beat me according to instructions which he issued from time to time interspersed with obscenities. I was struck by his calm. Almost reverie.

Sally This isn't good, mate. Not good at all. Rabe! Listen to me!

Rabe And everywhere dust.

Sally Worst bloody thing you've done. We're getting out of this kip. Now!

Rabe Hard wooden benches. Several broken. Also windows broken hanging cords of old blinds black with grime. Large table ink-spattered. So old. Names, cryptic messages, several of love or at least lust carved, seared, gouged out of the wood, there a long time, fading. Penknives used by prisoners, bits of razors other sharp instruments concealed about the person escaping body-searches. I saw people waiting in that room for centuries. That terrible waiting. Doors banging at a distance, feet on corridors. Also tattered posters, notices of fines payable by farmers with ragwort in their fields. Warnings about aliens and how to apprehend them. An old flag. Some proclamation of historical importance. They took me to pee in a yard in the rain. They stood around and watched.

Sally Right. That's it. Right. Clean you up. First things first.

Rabe I had been there before, you see. Different time. Different place.

Sally Belfast. We'll head towards Belfast.

Rabe There will always be that room, waiting.

Sally Now you listen to me, Rabe –

Rabe The room –

Sally No, you listen, lover! Cut the shit. You're not going to sink. Bloody self-indulgence, that's what it is.

Rabe It's not just me!

Sally Right. Sorry. I know. I know. Just look at me.

Rabe What? I don't even know you.

Sally Oh yes you do. And stop acting like a spoilt wane. Now. It's all gone. All gone. I'm going to talk you back, Rabe.

Rabe Talk me back –

Sally Right. Talk you back. You saw it in their eyes, right? You could smell it off their sweat and stink. You felt it rise with the heat off their bellies. You couldn't stop yourself. They said: We know who you are. We know what you are. We're going to get you, they said. And you said yes. Name me. Say my name. Call me what I am. Take me.

Rabe Take me.

Sally It's ended, Rabe.

Rabe Ended.

Sally All over. All burned out now. Nothing left. Time to move again.

Rabe Yes. (*Recognition.*) Sally!

Sally Merci beaucoup.

Rabe I feel utterly wasted.

Sally How're your legs?

Rabe Why?

Sally We're heading north.

Rabe Yes but why?

Sally (*rush*) Why because I've no wit. Because I'm a sucker. Because it's starting all over again. Until the next time, the next time. (*Rise.*) Because I want to go home! Because I love you you beautiful prick limey fucking lunatic and because I hope. Oh, yes, I hope. Can you walk? I mean walk. Miles.

Rabe My books! I must have my books with me.

Sally We'll get you your books.

Rabe Nothing else matters really.

Sally There's very little else to carry, anyway. Except your books.

They enter the van. **Jo** *emerges out of the darkness, watching the couple disappear. It is as if she has been secretly following, spying on them.*

Jo Rule number one. Never spend the night outside his window getting your death of cold hoping for a sign. I know I shouldn't be doing this. Besides he's with your wan. You don't have to tell me. I know all that. It's just I can't help it. I'm y'know, infatuated.

She begins to weep. Suddenly **Rabe** *jumps from the van carrying one or two small bags. He looks about apprehensively and then runs off into the darkness.*

Jo Rabe!

Sally *jumps from the van with even more bags.*

Sally Wait for me, Rabe!

She runs off after **Rabe**.

Jo Oh, Rabe!

Madame MacAdam *appears out of the darkness.*

Madame MacAdam I'm afraid he cannot hear you, my dear.

Jo They're really gone? Rabe and your wan?

Madame MacAdam I'm afraid they are.

Jo That's it so.

Madame MacAdam Do you feel better now?

Jo I think so.

Madame MacAdam I admire your pluck. You are a quick learner. Can you see the pictures in your head, my dear?

Jo Yes.

Madame MacAdam And do you see how they differ from what you perceive with your own eye?

Jo I think so.

Madame MacAdam Good. That is the first step towards lucidity. I abhor confusion. It is frequently offered as a substitute for living and a substitute for art whereas in fact it is simply failure. Never romanticize failure, my dear.

Jo When I told him I'd do anything for him I meant it. I can't make head nor tail of it. How can he just chop off something like that?

Madame MacAdam I'm afraid he has the need to do it. It's rather like an appetite.

Jo Do you mean he just walks away from people all the time?

Madame MacAdam I'm afraid so.

Jo That's sad for him, isn't it?

Madame MacAdam It's the source of his energy, alas. And of his creativity. He burns away everything each time to make a clean start.

Jo It must make him very empty, so.

Madame MacAdam He is constantly looking for the impossible, perfect performance. I told him he should confine his theatricality to the stage. I told him that that was the value of our acting. It is the nearest we can ever come to the essential. Even if we have to costume ourselves to do so.

Jo What are you trying to tell me, ma'am?

Madame MacAdam That you must take care of yourself, now.

Jo I don't care what happens to me any more after this.

Madame MacAdam Rubbish. One simply needs a tonic after a let-down.

Jo First the little Lannigan girl missing and now this. Do you think they'll blame me?

Madame MacAdam Men will blame us for anything, I'm afraid, from their performances in public to the condition of their dentures. That is not the point. The point is to be clear-minded and to be in touch with one's unique rhythm. The rest is chaos.

Jo I've a pain where my heart should be.

Madame MacAdam Place your hand on the spot! It is remarkable how ignorant people are of the exact location of the human heart. (*Looks at* **Jo**.) Yes, you would appear to know where it is! Now! Breathe in deeply. Allow the noxious vapours to excrete. Touch your extremities. Possess yourself! Possess yourself! You are unique and mistress of your fate. Believe that.

Jo I feel dizzy.

Madame MacAdam That is understandable when the full flood is upon you.

Jo It's what they did to him that I can never forget.

Bun Bourke *and his troop in full uniform appear across the back.*

Jo Oh, look! They're back again. What're they going to do?

Bun *leads his men smartly up and into the van.*

Jo What're they doing?

Madame MacAdam They are simply undressing. Casting off one role, putting on another. You mustn't be afraid, child. These are our demons. Pathetic, stunted, dangerous little men. I'm afraid that is another lesson to be learned from theatre. Once one puts on a uniform one is in danger of unleashing one's violence. Witness that slaughter out there on those battlefields. Boys performing at the behest of infantile old men. Though mind you I cannot understand this neutrality of yours here in Eirer. It obviously has little to do with pacifism, if the nocturnal behaviour of the natives is anything to go by.

Bun Bourke *and his men, tired and drooping, come out of the van dressed in their own work clothes. They drift away in a line.*

Madame MacAdam Tinker, tailor, soldier, spy. There they go!

Jo They shouldn't have beaten him like that so they shouldn't.

Madame MacAdam Back to normality. How dull it is! To live simply with one's wife and children! How fretful it makes the male!

Jo No-one should ever be treated like that, ever.

Madame MacAdam Sooner or later the itch will become intolerable again. On with the livery. And he will be able to kill again, wearing his insignia.

Jo I told him I would do anything he asked. And it's true I would.

Madame MacAdam (*pause*) Are you pregnant, child?

Jo I dunno.

Madame MacAdam Is it that you don't know how one becomes pregnant or is your uncertainty a matter of time passing?

Jo A bit of both, I think.

Madame MacAdam Have you no-one to talk to?

Jo No.

Madame MacAdam Do you understand your monthlies?

Jo I think so.

Madame MacAdam Come along.

Jo Where to?

Madame MacAdam Let us retire from this great stage of fools, my dear and chat about harmony.

Jo I don't know a thing about music.

Madame MacAdam I am not referring to music, child. I am speaking of the chambers of the body. One has to listen inwards. At a certain point of balance all is silence. Then one can re-emerge and face the mad tumult once more. Do you like chocolates?

Jo Oh I love chocolates.

Madame MacAdam I have a secret hoard for occasions such as this. But mum's the word. Mum's the word, now.

They go off. Hand in hand.

Race track noises off: bookies' calls, race announcements etc. The **Sergeant** *comes around the back of the van, very cautiously, wearing his police uniform and cap but carrying an old raincoat and cloth cap. He puts on this raincoat over his uniform and exchanges caps. He is stopped short by the sudden start of the race commentary and stands to listen.*

Race Commentary (*over*) Round the last bend Sheila's Fancy by a short head from Trusty Tess and Muckamore Lad Dixie's Wonder closing on the outside into the straight Muckamore Lad making ground, it's Muckamore Lad Muckamore Lad on the rails but here comes Dixie's Wonder! Muckamore Lad and Dixie's Wonder! Dixie's Wonder on the nose, Dixie's –

Roars from the crowd, off, boos and catcalls. The **Sergeant** *stands in a kind of awe, removes his cap, replaces it and rushes away. The sides of the van open up.* **Lyle Jones** *and* **Madame MacAdam** *pooled in light, very centre stage. He in crombie and velour hat, with greyhound* *on a leash, acknowledges the threatening shouts from the crowd, off, which is like an audience.* **Madame**, *in furs, is, slightly sinking, on his other arm.*

Madame MacAdam I have broken my covenant to accompany you here. What on earth persuaded me to do it?

Lyle Jones Petrol, darling and do keep smiling at these divine people, there's a dear.

He waves enthusiastically toward 'audience' off. Shouts and jeers: 'Go back to where ye came from, ye lousers!' 'Give us a look at that dog there, mister!' 'Hey, missus! What's yer name, missus?'

Madame MacAdam We are about to be ravished by the mob. What are we to do with this absurd canine?

Lyle Jones It is part of the subterfuge, darling. And do try to act as if we were dog people.

Madame MacAdam Dog people, indeed! Do you think we are on at the Hippodrome?

Shouts more menacing. Odd missiles, bits of paper, bread, fruit, hurled at **Lyle Jones** *and* **Madame**. *'Get the fuckers!' 'Robbers!' 'Where's our money!' 'That dog was switched so she was.' 'Get them!' 'Don't let them get away!'*

Madame MacAdam Lyle Jones! For Heaven's sake do something before we are trampled underfoot! We are engulfed!

Lyle Jones (*forward, great voice, Roman orator. There is immediate total silence*)
  Knowest thou me yet?
  You common cry of curs, whose breath I hate
  As reek a' the rotten fens, whose loves I prize
  As the dead carcasses of unburied men
  That do corrupt the air – What would you have,
  You curs? Hence! Begone!

Pause. Silence.

Madame MacAdam Good God! This is the final rending of the curtain. We have passed into another dimension!

Lyle Jones Did you see that? (*Off.*) See how they slink away! Curs! Churls! Caitiffs! You worse than senseless things! Gone! (*Down, conversational.*) How extraordinary! To triumph by actually emptying the house! Never did that before. Very peculiar. What does it mean?

Madame MacAdam Everything has gone into reverse. That's what it means! Can you expect otherwise when you have violated the very principle of theatre? Oh, Lyle Jones, where is your creative distancing, your discrimination?

Lyle Jones But, Mumsie, dear, I mastered the mob!

Madame MacAdam The same was true, I am reliably informed, of Mr Al Capone. Let us get out of here.

Slipper *runs on, furtively looking around him.*

Lyle Jones Attend! Here comes Autolycus, our very own picker up of unconsidered trifles. (**Slipper** *grabs the greyhound in his arms and makes off with it.*) What is this? Stop! (*Genuine grief.*) He has taken our dog!

Madame MacAdam Our dog! We-do-not-have-a-dog!

Lyle Jones (*off, after* **Slipper**) Come hither, boy! Just a tick! (*Further off.*) Bring back that dog!

Madame MacAdam Lyle Jones! He is gone. Useless, useless. He is incorrigible. Perhaps if I were a man I would understand what is happening. There is something terribly testicular about it all. Strutting about. Posture, posture. Action, action. Is it simply that men are by nature incapable of stillness? I shall walk all the way back to our humble lorry and begin to pack our few precious things.

She exits as the van closes up. The **Sergeant** *comes around the back of the van, removing his old raincoat, rolling it up, putting on his*

Garda cap. The figure of **Bun Bourke** *appears in the shadows. The effect should be of distance between them, a kind of haunting.*

Bourke (*one rush*) I didn't come down in the last shower no siree mister smart arse trying to pull wool over people's eyes and getting nowhere fast you and yer trick-actin' with that bitch of a dog beyond. Is it the dirt? I seen it, boy. Bun Bourke sees what is. They don't fool me with their fuckin' camouflage. Badge of duty hidden under the coat. Oh, ay! It'll be reported, boy, I'm tellin' ya that now, boy. Reported to the general below in Waterford. (*Disappears quickly.*)

Sergeant God Almighty what next? General? What general? Sure there isn't one general in the whole of the twenty-six counties of Ireland. Raving, raving.

Chamberlain, *with a fistful of money, on with* **Slipper** *and greyhound.*

Chamberlain Who're ya talking to, Sergeant?

Sergeant No one, Chamberlain, only myself.

Chamberlain Oh, don't I know the feeling well. (*Handing over cash.*) There y'are, Sergeant, more ten shilling notes than ya'll find in the Hospital Sweepstakes. No need to count it. From here on I'm a reformed man, Sergeant, amn't I right, Your Eminence?

Sergeant No, Chamberlain, keep it all.

Chamberlain What's up with ya?

Sergeant I can't touch it.

Chamberlain Ah, Jasus, Sergeant –

Sergeant The gambling, Chamberlain, the gambling! This time I'm finished with it entirely.

Chamberlain Listen, here, Sergeant. I'll tell ya about gambling, so I will. The world started crooked and we're all born to straighten it out. Do ya get me now? Sure isn't everyone that's anyone working overtime to correct the bias, to get rid of the warp, like? Am I right or am I wrong, Dr Einstein? Sure wasn't the first gambler Adam and his apple? And every time ya win one, Sergeant, you've put a shape on it the way it wasn't before. Do ya folla?

Sergeant Just leave me alone, Chamberlain.

Chamberlain Are ya sure?

Sergeant Sure I'm sure.

Chamberlain Come on so, Slipper and we'll take off the cosmetics offa yer ladyship there. (*Turns again.*) If ya only took half of it, Sergeant, ya'd only be hit by half of the distemper now? (*The* **Sergeant** *waves him away.*) Right, Slipper, we'll go home the back way. (*They exit.*)

Sergeant I've paraded my own town night and morning all my life sometimes on the bike, sometimes on shanksmare and do you know something for a fact? I never met anyone worse than myself. 'Tis I'm the criminal and not the misfortunates that I lock up. (*Lifts.*) Oh, but wasn't that a mighty performance by that man up there yelling at the whole crowd! And they all running away at the sound of his voice. Mighty is the only word for it!

Lights down.

Scene Six

Music. Projection: **The Death of Hamlet II. The Messenger Returns. Curtain Down and the World still at War.**

Madame MacAdam *alone on stage, folding and packing costumes and small props into a wicker hamper.* **Lyle Jones** *comes on carrying a regal costume and a crown in one hand.*

Madame MacAdam Is that the last of it?

Lyle Jones Don't you simply dread this part? Putting things away. Always reminds me of an auction. I detest auctions. Other people's things.

Madame MacAdam Let's not be dreary.

Lyle Jones I once knew an old actor –

Madame MacAdam Not now, darling, please –

Lyle Jones Yes, a dear old chap, always sang a hymn as he packed away his whatnots. Never asked him about it. Perhaps it wasn't a hymn? Can't remember any more.

Madame MacAdam Come along, now.

Lyle Jones I do have standards, you know. I do try to aim at the highest peak. Always have, all me life.

Madame MacAdam Yes.

Lyle Jones One is extremely bothered (*A vague gesture.*) by all this.

Madame MacAdam Lyle Jones, you have always been true to your own self. That's all that matters.

Lyle Jones It really is terribly kind of you to say that!

Madame MacAdam Now. Let us move onwards! (*Going off.*) Fetch the hamper along, will you?

Lyle Jones Yes. (*Alone, putting away the crown.*)
For God's sake let us sit upon the ground
And tell sad stories of the death of kings –

Pause. He closes the hamper and drags it back, straight into the following action: **Madame MacAdam** *is now sitting stonily in the front seat of the van. The* **Sergeant** *comes forward and helps* **Lyle Jones** *to stow the hamper into the rear of the van.* **Simon**'s *legs protrude from underneath where he is tinkering with the engine.* **Bun Bourke** *and* *some of his men oversee the departure.* **Marie Therese** *and* **Jo** *watch from the side.*

1st LDF Man (*to* **Bun Bourke**) Sure how can we push it with your man there stuck under it?

Bourke No back-answers. Orders is orders. Push! Get them out of here!

Lyle Jones (*to* **Sergeant**) I could become terribly attracted to the race-track, m'dear. All those little chaps running about with pieces of paper. Such brio, such elan!

Bourke (*to* **Sergeant**) I want them out of me district before nightfall and no buts.

Sergeant Is it you think you own the place?

Bourke I've made me contribution. (*He returns to his men.*)

Lyle Jones What is that chap's name in that rather fetching uniform?

Sergeant 'Tis time for ye to go.

Lyle Jones I am leaving part of myself here, Constable. But then that is true every night in the theatre.

Madame MacAdam (*without moving her head*) Lyle Jones!

Lyle Jones Hark! I am summoned! Firstly, I must speak of the boy Rabe. A word or two. Terrible cock-up. Please! I do not wish to point the finger. Last thing I want is – to point the finger. Truth is things always appear worse than they are. Know this myself in the business. Things said. Things done. Shouldn't be. Know what I mean, Sergeant? He is a decent chap, Rabe. Well, goodbye –

Sergeant Goodbye, sir. On behalf of the people of the town I would like to express our sincerest thanks and felicitations –

Lyle Jones Ah, the open road, Sergeant. The rising prospect before one –

Bourke (*to* **Simon** *underneath the truck*) Will ya get up outta that before we cut the legs offa ye! Did ya hear me? Get him out of there! Get him up!

Simon *disappears.*

Sergeant (*to* **Lyle Jones**) I have to say – you were great –

Lyle Jones (*modestly*) Oh, really –

Sergeant I've never seen anything like it.

Lyle Jones Well, we do try to please –

Sergeant It'll be remembered for ever –

Lyle Jones You are too kind.

Sergeant It was magic so it was.

Lyle Jones Oh, my dear man, you have filled my cup to overflowing – We may not be – how shall I put it – in the very first rank. Yet we have our dignity, sir. No. What is important in the end is that we make them *believe*, you see. Even for one moment. To *believe*.

Madame MacAdam Lyle Jones!

Lyle Jones Must go. Would simply love to stay. Sorry – eeeh!

Sergeant I'll say it in front of everyone. That's one of nature's gentlemen and no mistake, now.

Lyle Jones *is hoisted up into the rear of the van and the men get down to pushing.* **Lyle Jones** *suddenly springs back down again from the van.*

Lyle Jones Attention all! Important announcement. Spread it abroad. Bush telegraph. I shall perform my unique version of the Death of Hamlet, three nights a week, matinee on Saturday. Solo. One voice. Never before attempted on the stage. All parts played by the leading actor. Madame upon the pianoforte. Word of mouth. We are going on. Advise your neighbours. I have never failed to appear, you know. I always go on. No matter what the problem. Curtain up. Count the house. Then – speak!

A voice off, calling: 'Sergeant! Sergeant!' Enter **Young Maher**, *running.*

Young Maher They found her, Sergeant! They found her!

Sergeant Found who?

Young Maher The little Lannigan girl.

All to attention. **Madame MacAdam** *opens the door of the van and climbs down to join the others.*

Sergeant Who found her?

Young Maher The Reilly family found her.

Sergeant Found her where?

Young Maher She came walking out of the wood above at Coolabeg.

Sergeant She's alive?

Young Maher She's alive all right.

Sergeant How is she?

Young Maher She's caked with dirt. Her mouth is stained be berries. And her hair and clothes is stuck with briars and brambles. Some said she ate grass.

Sergeant God Almighty be thanked.

Lyle Jones Such a deal of wonder is broken out within this hour that ballad makers cannot be able to express it.

Bourke Shut up this instant, you!

Madame MacAdam *goes and embraces* **Jo** *and* **Marie Therese**.

Madame MacAdam This is a seed. I am returning to the mainland! To begin once more! (*She retires to the van as before.*)

Bourke (*to* **Lyle Jones**) Get into that fuckin' van this instant before I – come on. Get them outta here.

1st LDF Man We're trying! We're trying!

Bourke Push, will ye, push. Get them outta here.

The van has started to move. It goes offstage with much shouting and expletives from the men. **Jo** *and* **Marie Therese** *follow it, excitedly. A splutter of engine. Cheers. A roar of the engine. It's moving! We hear it go into the distance to offstage applause. The* **Sergeant** *is left alone. He looks around him, then practises one or two duelling feints with his blackthorn stick. Becoming bolder he puts on a little show. Then stops, embarrassed.*

A wild shouting offstage. The **Sergeant** *gapes. The* **LDF Men** *whooping and yelling come back on with a variety of stage-costumes, one of them pulling a costume-hamper, spilling clothing everywhere. As they pull on bits and scraps of costume they yell at one another: 'The hoor never saw it happen!' 'Jasus, will you look at that.' 'I nearly bust a gut, so I did.' ''Twas I got it out of the van.' 'Your man must be blind.' 'Look at Bun! Look at Bun.'* **Bun Bourke** *swaggers on, a crown on his head.*

Bourke See him! See King! See Majesty Michael, hah? Nice turnout, hah? Hey, boys? What do ya? Hah? We have 'em now, boys. Where'll they be now without their gee-gaws? Naked fuckers. Stripped.

Sergeant What's the meaning of this? Gather up them things.

Bourke Put a match to them.

Sergeant Leave those clothes there! D'ya hear?

Bourke Don't talk to me like that, mister.

Sergeant I'll talk to you anywhichway I want.

Bourke Will ya now? We have your measure, mister, in this town. We see through ya, boy. We're just waiting for ya to drop, boy. You and your fucking greyhounds.

Bun *throws away the crown. Gestures to his men who abandon the costumes. They drift, off. The* **Sergeant** *stands amid the debris, picking up the odd item.*

Sergeant (*handling costumes*) Lord save us but aren't they poor looking enough in the broad daylight! Would you credit it that people could be so fooled now? What'll they do now I wonder without their bits of covering and their hokery pokery? The misfortunates! I'll gather these up for safekeeping and just go home and turn the key in me own door and hope for the best.

Chamberlain, *followed by* **Slipper** *leading the greyhound, comes on and spots the* **Sergeant**.

Chamberlain Sergeant! The very man. Come here a minute. (*Looks around.*) I have a little proposition –

Sergeant No, no, no, Chamberlain – Not any more, please.

Chamberlain Hear me out, Sergeant.

Sergeant I don't want to hear a word of it.

Chamberlain But I haven't opened me mouth, amn't I right, Mr Dimbleby?

Sergeant I don't want to listen to it. (*Exits quickly.*)

Chamberlain You don't know what you're missing, Sergeant. Monte Carlo isn't in it!

Chamberlain *and* **Slipper** *follow the* **Sergeant** *off.*

Lights down.

Lights up: night light. The sound of a bomber approaching and passing overhead as in the opening of the play. **Marie Therese** *and* **Jo** *come out of the darkness with their bicycles.* **Marie Therese** *is looking up at the plane passing overhead.* **Jo** *is preoccupied, withdrawn into herself.*

Marie Therese I'd love to see your man up there, so I would.
You know the outfit they wear? I think it's gorgeous. The little
helmet and the goggles and the furry collar. Why do they wear
a furry collar, Jo?

Jo Because it's cold.

Marie Therese He's gone. Do you think it was the Jerries
or the Tommies, Jo? (*No answer.*) You're not mad at me, are
you, Jo?

Jo No. I'm not mad at you at all, Marie Therese.

Marie Therese I think you have nice hair, Jo. I really do. Do
you think the amusements'll ever come back again? Nothing
ever comes here to this place. Can you blame them? Daddy
says we'll all die here with the world passing by. Oh God, I'm
going to take the first boat to America, so I am. Do you really
think they'll come back, Jo? The amusement crowd? Jo?

Jo Oh, they will. (*Pause.*) Next year.

Lights down.